Deceptive Diagnosis
When Sin is Called Sickness

David M. Tyler, Ph.D.
and
Kurt P. Grady, Pharm. D.

Deceptive Diagnosis
When Sin is Called Sickness
by David M. Tyler, Ph.D.
& Kurt P. Grady, Pharm.D.

Scripture references are quoted from
The New American Standard Version of the Bible
and where noted,
The King James Version
and The New King James Version

Cover design by Melanie Schmidt

ISBN 1-885904-58-4

PRINTED IN THE UNITED STATES OF AMERICA
BY
FOCUS PUBLISHING
Bemidji, Minnesota

Foreword

I remember the first time I met Dr. David Tyler. We were both lecturing at a Biblical counseling conference in Alabama, and as I sat in the auditorium I watched as Dave electrified the audience when he spoke on the consequences of turning sin into sickness. I was impressed, not only with his message, but especially with his passion for the Word of God. I knew I had found a fellow soldier in the battle for biblical sufficiency.

At the same conference I also met Kurt Grady, a Christian pharmacist with strong convictions that psychotropic medications are over-prescribed for conditions that are primarily spiritual rather than organic. What a joy to find a medical professional who understands the consequences of psychological indoctrination and is willing to share his insights!

Since our initial meeting, I have been privileged to share time with these two gentlemen in a variety of settings and I have found that my admiration continues to grow. I have visited their Gateway Biblical Counseling Center near St. Louis and wish their ministries could be replicated across the globe as they train biblical counselors in cooperation with Master's Divinity School and the International Association of Biblical Counselors.

I believe you will find their book helpful as you examine the Church's growing tendency to pathologize every form of spiritual discomfort. It is written for pastors and laymen alike, and here's the reason: instead of seeking God's definitions and explanations of human behavior, more and more pastors, elders, and congregations are accepting a secular world-view which is based on humanistic psychology rather than the Bible. The result is an increasingly weakened Church, no longer certain of its message, mission and calling. Paul anticipated our day when he wrote, "See to it that no one takes you captive through hollow and deceptive philosophy, which depends on human tradition and the basic principles of this world rather than on Christ" (Colossians 2:8).

I encourage you to read this important book with an open mind. Ask yourself whether you *really* believe the Bible and are willing to trust our Heavenly Father, or if you have more confidence in the latest "findings" of psychology. Ask yourself whether you believe that sin is an actual problem that must be dealt with through the principles found in God's Word or whether all of life is a struggle with dysfunctions that must be solved therapeutically. Examine what is happening to the Church across America and around the world when people accept the disease model of human behavior. Learn how the mental health and pharmaceutical industries have joined hands to enslave mankind to a psychological world-view. Find out whether sin is caused by chemical imbalance or whether chemical imbalance and the resulting problems may be caused by sin. Ask yourself honestly, do I actually want to know? Your answers may well determine whether you will find lasting healing for your soul or a weak and miserable counterfeit that ultimately produces even more confusion.

I believe that if you will examine the arguments and evidence that Dave and Kurt provide in this book, your faith in God's Word and His power to transform lives will be strengthened. Your confidence to help others with their problems of living will be enhanced as you realize that our Lord is more than able to heal confused minds and wounded hearts. Remember, "…his divine power hath given unto us all things that *pertain* unto life and godliness, through the knowledge of him that hath called us to glory and virtue" 2 Peter 1:3 (KJV).

Dr. Ed Bulkley,
President, International Association of Biblical Counselors

Table of Contents

Chapter One
A Prescription for False Hope and Evil

The medical model of human behavior, when carried to its logical conclusions, is both nonsensical and non-functional. It doesn't answer the questions which are asked of it, it doesn't provide good service, and it leads to a stream of absurdities worthy of a Roman circus.

E. Fuller Torrey, M.D.
The Death of Psychiatry[1]

For a long time people have been led to believe that a person suffering from an excess of life's problems needs "expert" medical and psychotherapeutic intervention, thus allowing the "patient" to qualify for "illness"... Such a view is dangerous nonsense. If we are not ill, then we are well, although we may be unhappy.

Garth Wood, *The Myth of Neurosis*[2]

For all have sinned and fall short of the glory of God.

Apostle Paul, *Romans 3:23*

A New Vocabulary

Words can be powerful. They can inspire and they can comfort. Words can move us to action. They can calm a raucous crowd and quiet a frightened child. Words such as *"sola fide"* have shaped Christianity. A word such as *"freedom"* shapes our world. The words, *"That's one small step for man; one giant leap for mankind"* helped shape a generation. Words affect thoughts and behavior. Changing a word's usage can have far-reaching consequences. Consider the word "gay." Heard in conversation, its meaning 100 years ago was not the same as

1

it is today. Often, the impact of words on a culture is silent and slow. Sometimes the impact is considered positive, sometimes negative.

In the mid-1960's, a remarkable event related to a word occurred in evangelicalism. The event would have a devastating effect on evangelism and the sanctification of believers. Yet, in spite of the destructive consequences, this event went unnoticed by many Christians.

At that time, a major shift began in how evangelicals viewed and dealt with sin. The Church stopped calling sinful and deviant behavior "sin" and started calling it "sickness." The sexual sinner Paul wrote about (1 Corinthians 6:9) became a sex addict. The thief (1 Corinthians 6:10) became a kleptomaniac. The drunkard (1 Corinthians 6: 10) became an alcoholic. The rebellious child (2 Timothy 3:2) became afflicted with "Oppositional Defiant Disorder." A family in which the husband will not work, the wife will not keep the home, and the children will not obey is no longer considered sinful; it is dysfunctional. The liar became a compulsive liar. The gambler became a compulsive gambler. The idolater became a person who suffers from an obsessive-compulsive disorder. The "deeds of the flesh, which are immorality, impurity, sensuality, idolatry, sorcery, enmities, strife, jealousy, outbursts of anger, disputes, dissensions, factions, envying, drunkenness, carousing" (Galatians 5:19-21) have all been redefined using psychopathological words.

Placing sin in the category of sickness compromises the message of salvation. It sets aside the historical-grammatical method of interpreting Scripture and replaces it with a hermeneutic centered on pathology of the flesh. This interpretation views man as a victim who is sick rather than a sinner who is responsible to God. It eliminates the necessity for repentance. As such, the doctrine of the total depravity of man is undermined. Culpability and guilt vanish and there is no need for a Savior. In a similar way, sanctification is hindered. There is no need for repentance and change; no need for discipleship and spiritual growth. Believers are duped into thinking they are sick and need recovery. This explanation removes accountability. For example, if one has the flu, one is sick and misses work. No fault is assigned and one is not personally accountable for the sickness by one's employer. If the drunkard has a disease called alcoholism, he is no longer accountable for his behavior; rather, he is sick. It is not his fault. He has no need to repent; he needs twelve steps to recovery.

Sick people need recovery. Sinners need Christ.

The church today has lost sight of the fact that sin is the root of many problems and the source of many people's troubles. Biblical definitions and categories (the words) have changed and a new vocabulary related to disorders, "ism's", and chemical imbalances has emerged within the church. It is the vocabulary of humanistic psychology. Pastors and laymen alike are explaining the problems and difficulties of life in unbiblical terms like compulsions, addictions, phobias, dysfunctions and low self-esteem. Believers have absorbed the same "strange doctrines" of men that Paul warned Timothy about in his first letter (1:3), thus creating a new hybrid Christianity, nearly indistinguishable from psychology. The faith once delivered to the saints has been thoroughly mixed with the theories of Freud, Rogers, Adler and others. It is truly amazing how tolerable evangelicalism has become to bad theology! Christian men and women are more familiar with the psychological labels and jargon of our day than they are with Scripture. Pastors must realize that when they turn sin into sickness in the pulpit or in ministering to others, they are preaching "another gospel." Paul wrote:

> I'm amazed that you are so quickly deserting Him who called you by the grace of Christ, for a different gospel; which is {really} not another; only there are some who are disturbing you, and want to distort the Gospel of Christ (Galatians 1:6-7, NAS).

While the church has lost sight of the word sin, there are still glimpses of it from time to time. Sin has not completely disappeared from our vocabulary. Even "unreligious" people use the word in serious conversation. Christians still talk about *the* sin, in other words, Adam's sin that lead to the Fall and resulted in his expulsion from the Garden of Eden. However, there is little talk about personal sin and the depression, anxiety, fear, guilt and other feelings or physical symptoms they cause. For the most part, believers and unbelievers are more dignified and modern when it comes to talking about sin. After all, one does not want to run the risk of being labeled intolerant, insensitive, fundamental, or radical. One must be careful to use psychologically approved speech and language (words) that is (are) non-directive, non-judgmental, and non-offensive.

Worldly Words vs. Spiritual Words

The faculty of language and speech is one of the greatest abilities God gave to mankind. Although it seems ordinary, language is one attribute separating man from the rest of God's creation. Of all the things man does, speaking is one of the most important. The uniqueness of language is highlighted in God's revelation to man through His *Word*. Jesus Christ Himself is the Living Word. When God spoke and wrote, He raised language to a place of significance. Spoken and written language became the principal medium of truth. Through words, God revealed Himself. Through words, God reveals His plans and purposes. Through words, God defined, explained, and interpreted the world around Adam and Eve. God said to them:

> "Be fruitful and multiply, and fill the earth, and subdue it; and rule over the fish of the sea and over the birds of the sky and over every living thing that moves on the earth." Then God said, "Behold, I have given you every plant yielding seed that is on the surface of all the earth, and every tree which has fruit yielding seed; it shall be food for you; and to every beast of the earth and to every bird of the sky and to every thing that moves on the earth which has life, I have given every green plant for food"; and it was so (Genesis 1:27-30, NAS).

God spoke, but Satan spoke also. God's authority was challenged and His words were contested. The devil had a dramatically different way of explaining and interpreting Adam and Eve's world:

> Now the serpent was more crafty than any beast of the field which the Lord God had made. And he said to the woman, "Indeed, has God said, 'You shall not eat from any tree of the garden.'? The woman said to the serpent, "From the fruit of the trees of the garden we may eat; but from the fruit of the tree which is in the middle of the garden, God has said, 'You shall not eat from it or touch it or you will die.' The serpent said to the woman, "You surely will not die! For God knows that in the day you eat from it your eyes will be opened, and you will be like God, knowing good and evil" (Genesis 3: 1-5, NAS).

We live in a world where there are many interpretations of the same set of facts. One person looks at a butterfly and is moved by the splendor of God who created it. Another looks at the same butterfly and is moved by evolution's ability to make such a delicate insect. One man looks at a child's behavior and sees a sickness that is said to be caused by a chemical imbalance in the brain that could be corrected through the use of medications. Another man looks at a child's behavior and sees rebellion and sin.

It is not the facts (the child's behavior), but the interpretation of those facts (sin vs. sickness) at the core of the issue. Many explanations of life and the world do not recognize the authority of God and are, therefore, incompatible with a biblical worldview. *The right things are not said because the right things are not believed.* Adam and Eve listened to the serpent and believed an interpretation that was contrary to God's truth. From that point forward, the war of words has been raging. Today, Christians are listening to sinful man's (or the serpent's?) interpretation of the facts, rather than God's.

Christians are involved in the logical outgrowth of the war of words every day. It is the battle of ideas. While most believers, understandably, think of the battle in terms of its spiritual dimensions and "otherworldliness," we realize that there is an intellectual side to the battle that must not be overlooked. Paul wrote:

> Finally, be strong in the Lord and in the strength of His might. Put on the full armor of God, so that you will be able to stand firm against the schemes of the devil. For our struggle is not against the rulers, against the powers, against the world force of this darkness, against the spiritual forces of wickedness in the heavenly places. Therefore, take up the full armor of God, so that you will be able to resist in the evil day, and having done everything, to stand firm (Ephesians 6:10-13, NAS).

Paul goes on to write about the various elements of the Christian armor. There are the defensive pieces and one offensive/defensive piece; "the sword of the Spirit, which is the word of God" (v.17). If the Word of God can be neutralized in the life of a Christian, he is left with no offensive weapon for the battle. He is struck time and time again, yet he cannot strike back. To any military strategist or, for that matter, to anyone, the defensive strategy alone can be seen as a losing strategy.

The church has always been involved in a defensive battle involving ideas and words. These battles can be found all through the New Testament and Church history. There were debates about Jesus' identity and nature (Matthew 16:13). There were disputes over Christ's bodily resurrection (Acts 17:18). There were arguments as to whether a person must keep the Law of Moses in addition to faith in order to be saved (Acts 15:5).

In Paul's letter to Timothy, he spoke of his concern about worldly philosophies that were being taught at Ephesus (1Timothy 1:3). The battle of ideas and words continued throughout the centuries as one heretical idea arose after another. Conflicts of ideas and philosophies are what led the early church to organize its statements of doctrinal beliefs, such as the deity of Christ, personage of the Holy Spirit, the Trinity and so on. During the Middle Ages, perversion had crept into the church, and a battle of ideas concerning the purity of the New Testament and salvation by grace alone through faith alone in Christ alone was fought by the reformers.

In the eighteenth century, man became "enlightened" and optimistically believed his reasoning powers and scientific approaches would lead to a brighter future without God. In the nineteenth century, problems and challenges arose from Darwinism and Freudianism. Since the Church's inception, it has been in one skirmish after another with competing worldviews, ideas, and words.

A worldview is a set of beliefs that shapes the way a person views his world. It is the lens through which a person processes the events in his life. There is a biblical worldview, a naturalistic worldview, and so on. Every person has his or her own worldview. Thus, the correct worldview is very important in understanding words, ideas, events, and behaviors. Many disagreements among individuals stem from their differing worldviews. Atheists and Christians, Protestants and Roman Catholics, Calvinists and Armenians, and others have different worldviews. In each case, man has constructed a grid, as it were, that filters out certain ideas and arguments (words) leading him to a belief or an interpreted fact. Those whose worldviews differ often consider those with other views to be in error. Confused? Know this: God's Word is Absolute Truth!

Christians need to start thinking of Christianity not as a collection of bits and pieces of ideas to be believed, but as a complete, conceptual system - a total worldview, as it was originally designed. To break any worldview into disconnected parts will distort its true character. To mix certain parts of a worldview with a competing one leads to confusion and chaos. Each worldview carries its own assumptions. Each set of assumptions is, for the most part, incompatible with others. However, particular pieces of differing worldviews may be similar, like two slightly different circles that are superimposed. They are quite similar, but they are not easily reconciled. For example, two people with differing worldviews may both be pro-life or pro-choice. They may be similar in their politics or their morality. However, a significant problem occurs when major elements of conflicting worldviews are integrated. The result, eclecticism, is borrowing from a variety of worldviews, and is common practice in "Christian" counseling today.

A biblical anthropology, which teaches that man is made in the image and likeness of God, is combined with naturalistic-evolutionary anthropology, which views man as merely an evolving biological organism. The resulting eclectic integrationism, like purely secular psychology, calls sin sickness by mixing two antithetical worldviews. It is an attempt to be true to both worlds. Plainly, the integration of psychology with Christian theology by sincere but misguided believers has, in the Christian community, legitimized labeling sin as sickness. As a result, the Church has become convinced that the elaborate systems and theories, based on competitive worldviews, are a necessary addition and compliment to God's Word. The Apostle Paul condemns the integration of man's imaginary "wisdom" or worldview and God's true wisdom or worldview:

> Which things we also speak, not in words taught by human wisdom, but in those taught by the Spirit, combining spiritual {thoughts} with spiritual {words} (1 Corinthians 2:13, NAS)

Evangelicals have been habituated to think and speak psychologically. Biblical words, words taught by the Spirit, have been replaced by worldly words, words taught by human wisdom. God's true words, which are supposed foolishness, are exchanged for man's words, which are supposed wisdom. Words such as "kleptomaniac" and "alcoholic" (words taught by human wisdom) are misleading. They are euphemisms for sinful behaviors. The Bible never refers to a person as a kleptomaniac or an alcoholic. God's Word refers to a person who habitually gets intoxicated as a drunkard. A person who habitually steals is called a thief. In the sickness model, he needs recovery while in God's model, he needs to repent, put off the sinful habit, renew his mind, and put on the biblical alternative. Christians should use words taught by the Spirit as they accurately portray God's reality. The Apostle Paul wrote:

> See to it that no one takes you captive through philosophy and empty deception, according to the tradition of men, according to the elementary principles of the world, rather than according to Christ (Colossians 2:8, NAS).

"Rather than according to Christ" is the pivotal phrase Paul used to describe the system of doctrine (worldview) that had found its way to Colossae. It was a philosophy setting up the wisdom of man in opposition to the wisdom of God. "Man's wisdom," over the centuries, has taken many different forms, including the present-day sin-sickness movement. It has varied with time and culture, but it has always been present in one guise or another, to displace Christ's sufficient Word with man's wisdom.

Declaring People Sick

In the middle 1960's "illness" meant physical illness. The criterion for determining a disease was a change, alteration, or abnormality in the structure or function (anatomy or physiology) of the body as determined by invasive or non-invasive testing and/or a patient history and thorough physical examination. According to Webster's Comprehensive Dictionary, disease is defined as "disturbed or abnormal structure or physiological action in the living organism as a whole, or in any of its parts."[3] Abnormalities in these findings make it possible for a physician or pathologist to distinguish between the presence or absence of a disease. For example, a family physician takes a throat culture and discovers the presence of infectious streptococcus. A radiologist reads the result of an MRI indicating the presence of a brain tumor. A dermatologist takes a biopsy of a mole, sends it to the lab where a pathologist discovers no disease or abnormality. By using objective methods (throat culture, MRI, biopsy, and others) for discovering physical abnormalities, physicians can make a diagnosis. Abnormal anatomy or physiology dictates the presence or absence of disease.

Dr. Thomas Szasz, a psychiatrist and well-known critic of psychiatry and author of hundreds of papers and books, says of disease:

> "All too often the problem of defining disease is debated as it if were a question of science, medicine, or logic. By doing so, we ignore the fact that definitions are made by persons, that different persons have different interests, and hence that differing definitions of disease may simply reflect the divergent interest and needs of the definers."[4]

Szasz goes on to say:

> "...the decisive initial step I take is to define illness as the pathologist defines it...as a structural or functional abnormality of cells, tissues, organs, or bodies. If the phenomena called mental illness manifest themselves as such structural or functional abnormalities, then they are diseases; if they do not, they are not."[5]

There are constraints on a physician when he seeks to determine the presence of disease. In the past, a physician was constrained, bound, and limited to the scientific method. Disease was discovered based on objective tests. Under the new criteria in vogue today, instead of discovering disease by objective measures, a person can be declared sick based solely upon his complaint and the subjective opinion of the health care provider.

For example, one complains, "Doc, I've been having headaches for the past several weeks." The doctor replies, "You have a brain tumor. I need to operate first thing in the morning." You are shocked and you ask, "How do you know I have a brain tumor?" The doctor says, "You said you have headaches." In disbelief you reply, "But doctor, couldn't my headaches be caused by a sinus infection, low blood sugar, eye strain, stress, or lack of sleep?"

Would you let your physician perform brain surgery based solely upon your complaint and his subjective opinion? Of course not! Surgery is risky business. Taking medication for a declared mental condition diagnosed by subjective means is also risky business. When sin is called sickness, the boundaries and limits of good sense are removed and people are subjectively declared sick.

Today's diagnostic criteria say there does not have to be a change or abnormality in the structure of the body for a person to have a disease. If a person behaves badly, in a bizarre way, or fails to exercise self-control, they may be *declared* sick. After all, one who kills another has to be sick. Normal people do not kill or behave in wicked ways. At the core, there is good in every man, right? Wrong. (See Jeremiah 17:9). The Bible says Cain murdered Abel and God called it sin. David murdered Uriah and God called that sin. Jesus said, "For out of the heart come evil thoughts, murders, adulteries, fornications, thefts, false witness, slanders" (Matthew 15:19, NAS). Every one of those sins has now been declared to be a sickness. Jesus did not say out of a sick heart, but out of an evil heart comes sin.

The mental health industry has transformed the common everyday difficulties and hardships of life into declared diseases. A rebellious child has a conduct disorder. A person who overeats has an eating disorder. A person who is anxious or depressed has a mood disorder. There is adjustment disorder for the man who cannot seem to cope with his new job. The woman who is boastful and conceited has narcissistic personality disorder. The young man who repeatedly is arrested for destroying property, harassing others, or stealing is sick, too. He has antisocial personality disorder. Other conditions that may require clinical attention range from job dissatisfaction to religious issues such as questioning one's faith or values. People with common experiences of life are now damaged, wounded, abused, traumatized, and sick. They are by themselves incapable of dealing with their disease. It takes a trained "expert" to deduce psychological illnesses, to diagnose, categorize, and label the human experience.

We have allowed psychology to explain what we say, feel, and do. It interprets for us our words, moods, and actions, and what these really mean on an "unconscious" level. What one person says about an event of life and its effects are oftentimes interpreted by the psychologist into ideas which are very different from what is described. The psychologist then presents his diagnosis as fact, applies it to the person's situation, while transforming him into a victim and life-long patient.

The progression of events resembles the following:

1. A theory of victimization is constructed by the psychologist;

2. The theory is applied, using the esoteric language of psychology, to the person's situation;

3. The theory converts the person's experience into a disorder or disease;

4. Only the psychologist knows how to help provide relief;

5. Thus, a need for the psychologist is created.

Psychologizing or pathologizing, as some call it, turns routine experiences and feelings into abnormal conditions. Anxiety, apprehension, fear, sadness, and doubt are typically part of life's experience. Some become anxious when they ride an elevator or fly in a plane; others when they have to speak before a large group of people. Some may become fearful when driving in city traffic; others are fearful of the dark. While all of these may be annoying emotions and disturbing feelings and may disrupt life, they are, nevertheless, typical human experiences. However, to a psychologist, being anxious means something more. It means "having anxiety" or "having an anxiety disorder."

The mental health industry takes *authentic* victims of accidents, abuse, neglect, etc., and manipulates them into believing they are damaged and sick people. Traumatic life experience is turned into an ongoing emotional problem. The traumatic cause is often followed by a pathological effect. For example, the man, who after twenty-five years, is laid off from his job (the traumatic cause or experience) is later diagnosed with adjustment disorder (the pathological effect). A parent whose child dies (the traumatic cause or experience) is diagnosed with Post Traumatic Stress Disorder (the pathological effect). A person who was abused (the traumatic cause or experience) is diagnosed with Paranoid Personality Disorder (the pathological effect).

A TRAUMATIC CAUSE = A PATHOLOGICAL EFFECT

A traumatic cause leading to a pathological effect is accomplished by focusing on the negative and accentuating the trauma. The person now thinks of himself in terms of the distress or suffering he experienced. He is told that the experience has weakened him. To recover he must face the fact that the event was traumatic. He must then face it, confront it, and go through the psychological process which means changing himself from victim to survivor.

Real victims do not want to be victims at all. A woman who was raped would rather have not been raped. No one wants to be in a car crash. Pain, suffering, and loss are the consequence of being a genuine victim. No one wants to be assaulted and robbed. So why do people allow themselves to be categorized as psychological victims? Quite simply, there is an advantage to being made a victim. The psychological victim is given permission to live a psychologized life. Once diagnosed, he may step into another world. Being recognized as a victim of some major life trauma is the starting point in the journey where the therapist is viewed as the shepherd who will lead the victim to the promised land of recovery. What makes the future brighter for the psychologized individual is his victim status. The undiagnosed have to live with their disappointments, failures, regrets, crimes, and sin. The psychological victim's world is free from guilt, shame, and responsibility. Whatever the matter may be, an external cause is found for the damaging effects. The disease has removed the accountability that has, in turn, removed the guilt. As a corollary, it has also removed the need for a Savior or for the work of the Holy Spirit in sanctifying the believer.

Because Christians have become so indoctrinated with the sickness model, they unconditionally accept the diagnosis. Persons who are lazy, irresponsible, bitter, full of self-pity, mean, or immoral are *declared* to be sick. AIDS was discovered to be a disease. Alcoholism was *declared* a disease. Cancer was discovered to be a disease. Social anxiety disorder and pedophilia are *declared* to be diseases. When sin is called a sickness, behavior is labeled healthy or unhealthy as opposed to righteous or unrighteous. Drunkards are now in the same category as Alzheimer's patients. Rebellious children are in the same category as the man with heart disease. A murderer is in the same category as the cancer sufferer. And the man who gambles away his savings and loses his home to the mortgage company is in the same category as the little girl diagnosed with a terminal brain tumor.

It is not surprising that unbelievers would call sin sickness. The natural man does not accept the things of God, for they are foolishness to him (1 Corinthians 2:14). What is hard to believe is that the things of God have become foolishness to Christians. The Church itself has become an accomplice with the world in helping men justify their sin.

Men suppress the truth (Romans 1:18) when they call sin sickness. They exchange the truth of God for a lie (Romans 1:25). As James teaches, they are drawn away and enticed (James 1:14).

The whole idea of sin has always been hated by the world. Since Adam and Eve ran, hid, covered up, and shifted the blame in the Garden of Eden, man has been trying to justify himself. Calling sin sickness allows man to feel better. A healthy self-image is impossible if a man's heart is "deceitful above all things and desperately wicked" (Jeremiah 17:9, KJV). Or as Isaiah writes:

> "Behold, the nations are like a drop from a bucket, and are regarded as a speck of dust on the scales… All the nations are as nothing before Him, they are regarded by Him as less than nothing and meaningless" (Isaiah 40:15, 17, NAS).

The solution to these "destructive" words is that man rebels against, overrules, and turns upside down the Word of God. Behavior is reduced to chemical imbalances, electrical impulses, disease, or low self-esteem. Personal accountability for thoughts and behaviors is abdicated.

If there were such a thing as "corporate" multiple personality disorders, it would seem the Church has one. Out of one side of the Church's mouth, the Church says man is a sinner. Out of the other side of the Church's mouth, man is said to be sick. Is it possible to deny the doctrine of sin by calling sin sickness and still be preaching the Gospel of Jesus Christ? Sermons, Bible study literature, and books by beloved Christian authors are filled with euphemisms for sin. A fornicator may be called to repentance, but if he is sick then he is no sinner. Instead, he is an addict.

No Sin, No Guilt

If man is not a sinner then he is a patient who is suffering. He is a victim of the cruel and callous treatment of others. We are told that we must learn to be sensitive, tolerant, and compassionate, realizing the very behaviors we formerly labeled as sinful are now evidence of victimization or illness.

The culture we live in encourages all sorts of sinful attitudes and behaviors, but will not tolerate the guilt and other feelings that sin produces. Man does not exist in a vacuum. There are consequences to his actions. These consequences are part of the curse God put on man as a result of sin. Sinful behaviors and attitudes affect the way we think and feel. Sin can produce feelings of personal guilt, depression, anxiety, fear, and so on. For example, Cain's sinful behaviors lead to depression (Genesis 4:5-7). David experienced depression, anxiety, and several physiologic symptoms as a result of his sinful relationship with Bathsheba (Psalm 38). However, to admit responsibility and guilt is unsuited and irreconcilable with today's concept of human dignity and self-esteem. Guilt is therefore viewed as a "neurosis." It is an abnormal fixation that must be eradicated. Despite the incessant voice of one's conscience, the sinful behavior that causes us to feel guilty must be denied.

Sin as sickness has gained such a foothold in our thinking, there is no longer much thought of personal sin. We give a token recognition in sermons and conversations to what once was a strong and ominous word, but for the most part, has disappeared along with the whole notion of offending God. Have we ceased sinning? No, we are just calling it something else. Man, since the Fall, has become an expert at covering up his sin. Today, however, we are better equipped with psychological euphemisms for sin. Something is terribly wrong. By claiming the status of a sick person or victim, an individual can escape the responsibility of everything from murder to sloth. All kinds of immoral, perverse, and wicked behavior are now considered to be a symptom of some psychological disease. No one is responsible for these acts. People will admit they have vague feelings of personal guilt, anxiety, and depression, but no one has committed a sin. There are plenty of patients, but sinners are hard to find.

Christianity does not make sense without sin. The Church teaches, "God demonstrates His own love toward us, in that while we were yet sinners, Christ died for us" (Romans 5:8, NAS). On the other hand, the Church calls sin sickness. What's the truth? Is sin sin? If so, why does the Church sometimes call it sickness? If sin is sickness why does the Church sometimes call it sin? Is the Church really confused, or just embarrassed to use the word sin? Has fear of man made us ashamed of the gospel? Is the Church willing to trade biblical correctness for political correctness in order to be "seeker sensitive" and build staggering attendance numbers? Paul wrote: "If the trumpet makes an uncertain sound, who will prepare for battle? (1 Corinthians 14:8,

NKJV). There is definitely an uncertain sound coming from the pulpits of evangelicalism today. As a result, evangelism, discipleship and sanctification all suffer.

The apostle Paul was not ashamed of the gospel (Romans 1:16). The reason he was eager to preach in Rome was because the gospel was the way of salvation. The gospel was not some new philosophy of life. It is not some new idea, which can be interesting and absorbing to discuss and debate. No, the gospel is about deliverance from sin. Paul sets the gospel over and against the Greek culture, which had come to Rome years before. The study of philosophy is interesting, but it tends to begin and end with ideas of men. It ultimately leaves men where they started. Philosophy does nothing about sin. It does not save man from the guilt, power, and pollution of sin. It does not reconcile man to God.

Paul's letter to the Romans deals with fundamentals. With respect to systematic theology, the book of Romans is the most important book in the Bible. It has played a more important and more crucial part in the history of the Church than any other single book. Some of the Church's greatest leaders were converted while reading the Epistle to the Romans. For example, Augustine was saved while reading Romans 13. Augustine fought against the Pelagian heresy and defeated it by expounding the book of Romans. While he was still a Roman Catholic and a teacher of theology at the University of Wittenberg, Martin Luther prepared a series of lectures on the book of Romans. In doing so, his teaching of the doctrine of justification by faith through Jesus Christ and apart from works became a reality. John Bunyan and John Wesley also were converted to Christianity by means of this remarkable book.

Paul declared that God provides a way of salvation through faith in Jesus Christ. The question is why did God do that? Why did Jesus Christ leave Heaven, die on a cross, and rise again? The reason may be summed up in the following verse:

> For the wrath of God is revealed from heaven against all ungodliness and unrighteousness of men who suppress the truth in unrighteousness (Romans 1:18, NAS).

The most striking aspect of Paul's presentation of the gospel is that he begins with the wrath of God. Wrath refers to God's hatred of sin. If one recognizes the love of God, he must also recognize the hatred of God. All that is opposed to God is hateful to God. Paul said that God's righteousness has been revealed (Romans 1:17), making the following verse, "For the wrath of God is revealed… against all ungodliness and unrighteousness of men," quite inevitable (Romans 1:18).

Therefore, Paul does not begin the gospel presentation with man and his problems, but with God, who is angry having been offended by sinful men. He does not say he is ready to preach the gospel to them because they are living defeated and troubled lives and the gospel will lift them out of their depression. He does not say he is ready to preach the gospel because they are unhappy and the gospel will make them happy again. He does not start with man's troubles and difficulties. He does not start by telling them that he has had a wonderful experience and wants them to have it too. Paul starts by talking about the wrath of God against all men because of sin. The wrath of God against sinful man is the motive for evangelism.[6]

Mixing Christianity and psychology has created a climate in which the word sin has been diluted of its true meaning and has been rendered harmless. If an unbeliever has no consciousness of sin, he will not be able to see the point of Christianity. To him, Paul's statement concerning the wrath of God will not make sense. This is not only true of unbelievers, but also Christians. Many Christians have lost their consciousness of sin. It is considered harsh, insensitive, or even "un-Christian" to speak of problems as being the result of sinful behavior. No one wants to hear he is a sinner. There is great comfort in being told problems are caused by a disease, disorder, chemical imbalance, addiction, repressed memories, phobia, low self-esteem, or a painful past. To many, the problem is how to market the Church in a way that will bring it in line with the latest intellectual and cultural beliefs while not compromising biblical integrity. The goal is to bring more people under the preaching of the Gospel. Psychology, they thought, was one way to give Christianity a "scientific" relevance and make it more attractive. Proponents of psychology insist it actually improves Christianity. Sadly, biblical integrity and, therefore, the Gospel, have been enormously compromised. The Church's fear of irrelevance in the postmodern world has lead to uncritically accepting man's wisdom and denying God's.

Meanwhile, the Church has become weakened and has experienced a dramatic decline in conversions over the past several decades. Church leaders are falling all over one another trying to do all they can to make the Church "relevant," and to give it purpose. Christian leaders speak of the "assured results" of a seeker friendly atmosphere, contemporary music, and so on. If one of the problems is calling sin sickness, then nothing short of a return to the language and intent of the Bible will rectify the problem. Sinful people need to repent and follow God's prescribed plan rather than relying on a prescription for a medication to treat their feelings.

The point of Christianity is that man sinned and Christ died to reconcile him before a righteous and holy God. Christians throughout history have been motivated to evangelize by their conviction that the Gospel of Jesus Christ is true. It has created in them a sense of urgency to go tell others. Paul wrote:

> I am under obligation both to Greeks and to barbarians, both to the wise and to the foolish. So, for my part, I am eager to preach the gospel to you also who are in Rome (Romans 1:14-15, NAS).

and

> For the love of Christ controls us, having concluded this, that one died for all, therefore all died; and He died for all, so that they who live might no longer live for themselves, but for Him who died and rose again on their behalf (2 Corinthians 5:14-15, NAS).

It was the love of Christ in Paul, combined with the conviction that what Christ did was complete and necessary for the redemption of all men, that produced the urgency motivating him to ministry.

How do we begin the task of communicating the Gospel to a society believing sin is sickness? Tell them the big story. Begin with the creation and the first man and woman. Explain the first act of rebellion toward God and the curse that God placed on mankind as a result. Continue through the Old Testament with Cain, Abel, Abraham, Isaac, Jacob, David, and so on. Step by step, establish in them a biblical worldview with the intent to introduce them to Jesus Christ. Effective evangelism has always been accomplished using key passages and verses that deal with sin, grace, and faith. The point is found in the death and resurrection of Jesus Christ. It does not matter whether one is preaching or teaching from the Law, the prophets, the historical books, the wisdom literature, the Gospels, or the Epistles; they all point to the Lord Jesus Christ, who died for our sins.

The landscape of evangelicalism today is very disturbing. Christians have jettisoned their commitment to God's sufficient Word. A psychological Tower of Babel has been erected. Biblical definitions and categories have changed and a new vocabulary has emerged within the Church. Behaviors and attitudes once regarded as sinful have undergone a dramatic change. They have been reappraised. Sin is called sickness. Confessing sin has been replaced with recovering from sickness. The word "sin" has nearly disappeared from our vocabulary. As such, the impact of the Gospel to a non-believer is less pronounced and the need for progressive sanctification in the believer is minimized. Nevertheless, there is, in the back of our minds, the fact that sin is still with us - somewhere, everywhere. It is a vaguely uneasy feeling. Although we try to make ourselves *feel* better by calling sin by another name, it is always there. It never fully goes away.

Notes

1. E. Fuller Torrey, M.D., *The Death of Psychiatry* (Radnor, PA: Chilton Books Company, 1974), p. 24.
2. Garth Wood, *The Myth of Neurosis* (New York, NY: Harper & Row Publishers, 1986), p.1.
3. Marckwardt AH, Cassidy FG, McMillan JB (eds.) *Webster Comprehensive Dictionary. International Edition.* (J. G. Ferguson Publishing Company, 1992, Volume 1), p. 365.
4. Thomas Szasz, *The Idea and Its Consequences.* (New York, NY: John Wiley and Sons, 1987), p.17.
5. Ibid., p. 12.
6. Throughout the New Testament the starting point when declaring the gospel is the wrath of God. For example, the first thing John the Baptist said to the people that came to hear him was they should repent of their sins and "flee from the wrath to come" (Matthew 3:7). Peter on the Day of Pentecost preaches concerning men's relationship to God. The sermon would affect them in such a way that they cried out "Brethren, what shall we do?" (Acts 2:37). Paul's sermons throughout the book of Acts emphasize man's relationship to God and the judgment that will come because of sin (13, 14, 17, and 20).

Chapter Two
Sin Really Does Matter

Abandoning the language of sin will not make sin go away. Human beings will continue to experience alienation, deformation, damnation, and death no matter what we call them.

Barbara Brown Taylor, *Speaking of Sin,*
The Lost Language of Salvation[1]

We cannot avoid facing the riddle of original sin itself. We have observed that the doctrine, as stated and unfolded, sheds light on the human predicament.

Henri Blocher, *Original Sin,*
Illuminating the Riddle[2]

When Jesus heard it, he saith unto them, They that are whole have no need of the physician, but they that are sick: I came not to call the righteous, but sinners to repentance (Mark 2:17, KJV).

The New Evangelism

In 1946 the federal government took responsibility for promoting the mental health of Americans. Some of the initiatives included the National Mental Health Act (1946), the National Institute of Mental Heath (1949), the National Mental Health Study Act (1955), and the creation of the Joint Commission on Mental Illness and Health (1955). The landscape of American society would be dramatically transformed with the building of new mental health centers, the incorporation of training programs as well as countless locations disseminating mental health principles. On February 5, 1963, President John F. Kennedy delivered a national speech on mental health. He referred to mental health as the nation's number one health problem. In order to confront what was considered a mental health care crisis, Kennedy signed

---

into law the Community Mental Health Centers Act on October 31, 1963. The diseasing of America and calling sin sickness now had the backing of the federal government. In 1977 President Jimmy Carter organized the Commission on Mental Health. The agency studied the state of the nation's mental heath and concluded a quarter of all Americans needed mental health services. In the 1980's an eruption of twelve step programs provided a disease label for virtually anyone who wanted one. The television talk shows capitalized on and added to the success and growth of the disease model. From Donahue to Oprah, common everyday people and celebrities alike would pour out their heart-wrenching stories of codependency and other addictions, disorders and compulsions. No segment of society was exempt. Therapeutic holidays such as National Depression Screening Day, National Anxiety Disorder Day and National Eating Disorders Awareness Week were created. Local malls provided a convenient venue on these special days where people could be diagnosed and learn more about their disease. For those who were too busy to go to the malls, a program of mental health education and screening for early detection and intervention became available online or by telephone.

Out of this milieu came one of Satan's master strokes of deceit. The entire landscape of America had changed. Rich or poor, black or white, male or female, all believed happiness and feeling good was the end and psychological healing was the means. The Church, not wanting to be left behind and cast as irrelevant, jumped on the bandwagon of the new faith. Convinced of psychology's scientific status, sin was whitewashed and attributed to disease. A therapeutic gospel was born where feelings, happiness, self-esteem and psychological healing were sacred. Mental health education was incorporated into ongoing Church programs. Support and recovery groups claiming to be Christ-centered became the new evangelism. Conversions in main-line denominations have been falling ever since.

The psychiatric community has long recognized the Church's potential influence among its members and others in the community, and therefore the strategic position of the Church is to advance the "health-engendering" philosophies of psychology. Today the Church of Jesus Christ is one of the nation's leading disseminators of mental health principles. Promoting mental health, through countless support and recovery programs, has become a vital ministry of the local

Church. The emphasis and driving force is a belief that spiritual and mental health is inseparable. During the years of modern psychology and psychiatry there was a compartmentalization of the spiritual and psychological. The Lord Jesus Christ said the greatest commandment was to love God and the second was to love neighbor. Today's wisdom says that people who are mentally ill have an impaired ability to give and receive love; thus helping them to recover from their disease has spiritual implications.

The Language of Disease, God's Love, and Grace

The Church's devotion to psychology has led to many additions and subtractions to the language of faith. The argument is, since science has provided us with new insights into human nature, the old words simply do not work anymore. Words like damnation, repentance and sin when spoken out loud sound dreadfully inappropriate. They are words from an earlier time when man's relationship with God was associated with guilt and punishment. They are words that judge us and leave us feeling uncomfortable, anxious or depressed. For far too long the Christian message (i.e. words) is said to have been distorted in ways that cause emotional hurt rather than healing. Howard J. Clinebell, Jr. wrote: "Through the centuries, religious leaders have been handling psychological dynamite with little awareness of the tremendous power for good or ill in their hands."[3] He went on to explain how behavioral science has given us a "fresh revelation of man", which has been extremely beneficial in helping us to interpret the Christian message in a way that will not do psychological harm.

The obvious solution is not to use the psychologically harmful words. That is exactly what has happened. Ministers are encouraged to check their sermons against mental health criteria for dangerous language. One pastor said it was helpful to him to interact with a professional therapist in his congregation before preaching some of his sermons. Other pastors, who do not have a mental health professional to consult with, glean "wisdom" from the books of famous Christian and secular psychologists and psychiatrists. Whatever the situation, sin-talk is out and the focus is on "disease", God's love and grace. Love and grace are said to be more positive and life-affirming. However, discarding the language of sin weakens and softens the full impact of grace. The grace of God is cherished most by those who realize their sinfulness most. The parable of the prodigal son illustrates the point.

The Scriptures said the prodigal son "came to himself" (Luke 15:17). He had been unconscious of his true condition; in other words, his sin. He had replaced bitter for sweet and sweet for bitter, darkness for light and light for darkness. It was as if he had been in a sinful trance and now he was awakened. All boasting of his supposed rights and claims were gone. He had been full of pride, but now he was humbled and had given up all ideas of self-justification. He could only hope to be treated as a hired servant. And so, full of shame and remorse, he began his long journey home. When his father saw him coming he wept within himself to think that his son was in such a pitiful and haggard condition. His eyes were sunken in their sockets and his checks were hollow from malnourishment. His clothes were rags. He was nothing but skin and bones. The Scripture described their reunion in verse 20. "His father saw him and felt compassion for him, and ran and embraced him and kissed him." The son, filled with shame, scarcely dared to think of embracing his father, but his father ran to embrace him.

The prodigal son confessed, "Father, I have sinned." His father said to the servants, "Quickly bring out the best robe." The son said, "I am no longer worthy to be called your son." His father said, "Put a ring on his hand and sandals on his feet." The son said, "Make me as one of your hired men." The father joyfully declared, "Bring the fattened calf, kill it, and let us eat and celebrate." Each gift was a token of his father's love and forgiveness. The son was guilty. He knew he was guilty and deserved nothing but his father's retribution. It was his guilt that heightened his awareness of his father's goodness and love.

When one realizes that he has sinned the stakes go up dramatically. Sinning sounds much more serious than saying, "I have a made a mistake, a poor choice or I have an obsessive compulsive disorder." Blame shifting is a common practice dating back to Adam and Eve. Adam blamed Eve, she in turn blamed the serpent and so on. We are all experts at dodging responsibility for sin. "I am a drunkard, says one man, because my father was a drunkard." Another bemoans his anger and the problems it has caused his marriage and blames his mother who was an angry woman.

Paul wrote, "For one will hardly die for a righteous man; though perhaps for the good man someone would dare even to die. But God demonstrates His own love toward us, in that while we were yet sinners,

Christ died for us" (Romans 5:8). One may conceivably be persuaded
to die for a good man; that is, good in human terms. In God's estimate
all are useless and have turned aside into rebellion. Paul wrote, "There
is none righteous, not even one" and "There is none who does good"
(Romans 3:10, 12). Christ died for neither the righteous nor the good, but
the ungodly. His dying transcends all human instances of self-sacrifice
for others. His dying is all the more wonderful and amazing in that it
proves His love beyond what is common among men.

Sin matters. Grace and forgiveness can only be adequately
experienced and understood when man's wickedness and sin is
understood. The goodness and mercy of the prodigal son's father
could not be understood apart from the son's rebellion and rejection
of the father. It is a story of sin and grace. It is not just a story of a
merciful and good father. It is also about a rebellious son. Peter wrote
in his first epistle, "But you are a chosen people, a royal priesthood,
a holy nation, a people belonging to God, that you may declare the
praises of him who called you out of darkness into his wonderful
light" (2:9). The wonderful light can only be comprehended when
one knows darkness. Therefore darkness is our only hope of knowing
light. Sin is our only hope of knowing life-giving grace. Men will not
know their need for grace and mercy apart from knowing their sin.
The crucifixion, the crowning act of mankind's wickedness, was God
the Father's crowning example of grace. It was sin's most infamous
moment and grace's supreme moment! In man's most wicked deed
we see God's most gracious act.

Sin and grace are both greatly magnified in the story of the woman
who washed and anointed Jesus' feet:

> And there was a woman in the city who was a sinner;
> and when she learned that He was reclining at the
> table in the Pharisee's house, she brought an alabaster
> vial of perfume, and standing behind Him at His feet,
> weeping, she began to wet His feet with her tears,
> and kept wiping them with the hair of her head, and
> kissing His feet and anointing them with the perfume
> (Luke 7: 37-38).

While some confuse her as being Mary Magdalene or Mary of
Bethany, most agree that she is neither. Her name is not mentioned.
The woman was distinguished only by the title of "a sinner." However,
she was not just a sinner in a superficial, every day sense of the word,

but a sinner in the blacker, despicable and filthier sense. She was a well known sinner. She was a sinner marked and labeled because Simon immediately recognized her as one of the town's many prostitutes. Persons of decent character would not associate with her. Like a leper she was cut off from society. However, she was the object of grace.

The story begins with the woman hearing that Jesus was at the house of Simon. Earlier in the chapter Jesus had been preaching to the people. Perhaps it was then, attracted by the crowds, she first heard the good news. As Christ spoke of the abounding mercy and willingness of God to accept as many as would come to Him, the tears ran down her cheeks. She became a new woman, desirous of better things, anxious to be freed from sin. She truly believed Jesus of Nazareth was the Messiah who had come to earth to forgive sin. She rested on Him for the forgiveness of her sin. However, there was still the nagging question: could she, would she, truly be forgiven? She did have faith, however feeble, and desired an opportunity to pay Him homage and possibly receive a word of assurance and confirmation.

When she learned He had come to her town she thought, "here is my opportunity." And so, uninvited, she entered the house of Simon. When she came through the door Jesus was reclining at the table (according to the Oriental custom) and His feet were toward the door. She had noticed Simon had not paid Christ the ordinary courtesy of washing His feet. This broke her heart. With all sensitiveness of her sinful past she began to wash His feet with her tears and wiped them with her hair. Her beautiful hair, her chief adornment that attracted many men for sinful purposes, was the means of service to the Son of God. She was as penitent as she had been a sinner. Love and grief was mingled together in her actions. First, she thought of her wicked life and then she would think of His grace and mercy. She kissed His feet. She took an alabaster vial filled with a costly perfume, which she had undoubtedly purchased to anoint herself and enhance her beauty, and poured it upon His blessed feet. She did not say a word. Her actions proclaimed her gratitude with a loud voice. Jesus defended and praised her to the self-righteous Pharisee. Jesus said to Simon, "Her sins, which are many, have been forgiven, for she loved much; but he who is forgiven little, loves little." Turning to the woman He said, "Your sins have been forgiven." The Lord's words sealed her pardon. From that day on she had full assurance of faith.

Grace gives attention to the most unlikely cases in order to show it to be grace. Grace finds a dwelling place in the most unworthy heart that its freeness might be better seen. Grace removed brazenness from her face flattery from her lips, and lustful desires from her heart. And though she had been recently awakened of her sinful state she did not comprehend all the heinousness of her guilt. Jesus allowed her to wash His feet with her tears even though He knew of the shameful things her eyes had looked upon. Our Lord permitted her lips to kiss His feet even though He knew the foul and licentious words that had come from those lips. He knew her heart had been full of unhallowed and unchaste desires for He spoke of "her sins which are many" (v: 47). The Savior knew her best and yet He did not cast her away. He did not move His feet. He did not rebuke her. He was delighted and refreshed by her sense of sin and grateful sense of forgiveness.

It is self-evident: there can be no grace where there is no guilt. There can be no mercy where there is no sin. If man is not a sinner then God cannot show mercy or pardoning grace toward him. It is ridiculous to talk of forgiveness when no wrong has been committed. It is a misuse of words to speak of bestowing undeserved favor upon a person who deserves reward. It would be an insult to an innocent person to offer him mercy. One must have sin or one cannot have grace. Leaving grace out of the story will ultimately lead to legalism, empty ritual, and men trying to earn what can never be earned. On the other hand, grace rings hollow, insignificant and trivial without sin. Sin and grace: one cannot be understood or measured without the other.

Today the language of sin is said to be depressing and counter-productive to one's mental well-being or self-esteem. Man, by nature, wants something to make him feel better. The language of love and grace is calming and supportive. It domesticates God and turns Him into a sympathetic and benevolent grandfather who encourages us when we are "sick" or sad. The price we pay is genuine grace. The language of grace requires a vocabulary of sin. However, to admit to sin is to confess something is wrong with *you*. It implies willful rebellion against God. It evokes feelings of responsibility, guilt and judgment. The apostle Paul said all men are "by nature children of wrath" (Ephesians 2: 3). We are not born neutral. We are not evenly balanced with the possibility of going either way, good or bad. Man is evil. For example, David analyzed himself and was awakened to his wicked behavior (Psalm 51). He committed adultery with Bathsheba and murdered her husband to cover up his crime. How could David, a man after God's own heart, do such a thing? What made him capable of such vile and horrendous actions? There is only one answer as he wrote, "Behold, I was brought forth in iniquity, and in sin my mother conceived me" (v: 5). David refers to his conception and birth with the clear understanding that his very being is permeated with the tendencies that produced the fruits of adultery and murder.

Slavery to Sin

Something is terribly wrong with the world. When one looks at the basic and fundamental problems of life and living, is it not obvious that the world is in a terrible state? The widespread and pervasive occurrence of human evil cries out for explanation. Oswald Chambers wrote:

> When we read the history of the race, our thoughts must fit into one of two fundamental categories: either we are wonderful beings in the making or we are wonderful ruins of what we once were. The latter is the view of the Bible.[4]

What is wrong? Since the world is not self-explanatory, an explanation must be sought from its Maker. Without His assurance and clarification the world appears to be full of absurdities and contradictions. The Creator says man is a sinner. The doctrine of Original Sin and its transmission has always been a Christian assessment of reality. Sin is why people do what they do. Every day experience heightens its relevance. On one hand, we boast of the great progress that man has made; his knowledge and achievements. On the other hand, there is this tragic breakdown in personal relationships. It is one of society's major moral and social problems. In spite of the fact that there are more institutions and organizations than ever giving new information and instruction, problems persist. For instance, there are available today countless books, classes and seminars on marriage. Up until a few decades ago men and women were married without this expert advice. A collapse of relationships between one group and another group has resulted in industrial and economic problems. On even a higher level, there is the relationship between nation and nation. The threat of war is always present somewhere in the world. This is proof that there is something wrong with the world. It is proof that man has fallen.

The inclination is to lose sight of the fact that we are sinful apart from our actions. Sin is not just separate acts of the will. Sin is in us. It is part of our very nature. Jesus said, "For out of the heart come evil thoughts, murders, adulteries, fornications, thefts, false witness, slanders" (Matthew 15:19). The trouble is with man's heart. Paul said, "For I know that nothing good dwells in me" (Romans 7:18). Man himself is corrupt. The Bible tells us repeatedly sin is not just wrongdoing, it is wrong-being. When men look at sin psychologically, sin becomes defective development or disease. Sin is not a disease nor is it something we catch in public. Though it is inherited, sin is not genetically manifested like cystic fibrosis or Tay Sachs disease. Sin is within man's nature and his nature is sinful. Man's intellect can never fill in the gaps that only God can provide. The Bible speaks of man's sinful disposition or heart. It is the heart of man that the atonement addresses:

> And I will give them one heart, and I will put a new spirit within you; and I will take the stony heart out of their flesh, and will give them a heart of flesh (Ezekiel 11:19).

> Cast away from you all your transgressions, whereby ye have transgressed; and make you a new heart and a new spirit: for why will ye die, O house of Israel? (Ezekiel 18:31).

> A new heart also will I give you, and a new spirit will I put within you: and I will take away the stony heart out of your flesh, and I will give you a heart of flesh. (Ezekiel 36:26).

The trouble with modern statements concerning sin is that they make sin far too trivial. Sin is a mistake, an imperfection, an error, someone else's fault, broken neurotransmitters or low serotonin. Committing sin is easy, while confessing it is difficult. A man will sin without a tempter, but he will not acknowledge his guilt no matter how much he is begged. Although his sins stare him in the face he still pleads his innocence. He proudly lifts up his head, challenges his accuser and rebuts responsibility. He argues had it not been for extenuating circumstances or providence itself he would have not been compelled to sin. Aaron, when confronted by Moses concerning the golden calf, acted as if his sin was an accident. Aaron said the people gave me their gold and "I threw it into the fire, and out came this calf" (Exodus 32:24). Saul ignored the instructions of Samuel the prophet and offered a burnt offering. Saul shifted the blame to Samuel, whom he accused of being late, and the people, whom he accused of getting restless. Saul said to Samuel, "So I forced myself and offered the burnt offering" (1 Samuel 13:12).

Sin, culpability and guilt are hard to determine in a world where people color and cloak their sin in all kinds of psychological language. Is she a shoplifter because she is willfully sinful or does she have kleptomania? Is the child willfully selfish or does he have Attention Deficit Hyperactive Disorder? Is he an arsonist or is he a victim of pyromania? Does he need a pastor or a psychiatrist?

Theologians over the centuries have spoken metaphorically of sin as an infection, infirmity or disease. While the metaphor may be helpful and descriptive, it may also be very seductive. Losing sight of the metaphoric distance between sin and sickness is an imaginary reality in evangelicalism of our time. Disease may be very similar in some ways to sin and sin to disease, but they are not the same. The phenomenon of "slavery to sin" does, in fact, exist. One may, as is the practice today, call slavery to sin a sickness, but there are reasons why you should not do so. For example, the opportunity to sin is often seen as being exciting and pleasurable; sickness is not. Men do not pursue multiple sclerosis or streptococcus the way they pursue adultery (James 1:14-15; 1 John2:15-17; Titus 3:3; Hebrews 11:24-26; 1 Corinthians 10:6; Ephesians 2:3). People become infected with diseases not because they want them, but because of a bacteria or virus. People in sin often seek ways to justify continuing in their conduct; however, no one tries to justify continuing a disease. Unlike disease, sin is something we can avoid and overcome (1 Corinthians 10:13; Philippians 4:13; James 4:7; 1 Peter 5:8-9; Ephesians 6:1-18). People involved in sinful behavior often encourage others to participate in the activity with them (Genesis 3:6). People don't encourage their friends to get cancer or arthritis. God punishes people for their sin. People are not punished for physical diseases which are beyond their control. The Bible teaches that an individual can choose to repent and put off his sinful behavior. No one has the ability to simply quit having influenza.

Slavery to sin is apparent in that, after sinning over a period of time, people will find their sin no longer pleasurable. Nevertheless, they may continue to sin in the same way. They have become habituated to the sinful behavior. They are "hooked" and find it very difficult to quit. It is this aspect of behavior that in some way makes it feel like a disease. The disease metaphor can be useful because it emphasizes the way one can feel controlled by something other than one's own will. However, the disease metaphor ignores the Biblical teaching of man's bondage to sin which is rooted in his relationship to Adam. Sin entered the world through Adam and affected his posterity making them sinners (Romans 5:12-21). The disease metaphor also overlooks the fact that the bondage man may experience is intentional and willful. Sin's mastery over man is voluntary. The preference of sinners is to give themselves over to their desires. They choose slavery to sin. Sin is not part of DNA. Adam and Eve sinned in the garden and their DNA was perfect. Lucifer, an angel, sinned prior to the foundation of the world and he has no DNA. Thus, while sin is the cause of all sickness in the flesh, sin is not embedded in man's DNA. Sin is the result of our capacity, being made in the image of God, to think in abstract terms and to exercise our fallen will over God's perfect instructions for living and behavior. A perfect example is addiction.

Addiction: Sin or Sickness

> *Every major tenet of the "disease" view of addiction is refuted both by scientific research and by everyday observations. This is true even for alcoholism and drug addiction, let alone the many other behaviors that plainly have little to do with biology and medicine.*

> Stanton Peele and Archie Brodsky,
> *The Truth About Addiction and Recovery*[5]

The growth of addiction treatment, based on the idea that alcoholism and addictions of all kinds are diseases, has spread like a wildfire throughout America. All sorts of recovery and self-help programs such as Gamblers Anonymous, Emotions Anonymous, Overeaters Anonymous, Debtors Anonymous, Depressives Anonymous, Impotence Anonymous, Grief Care, Women Who Love Too Much and others have sprung up in churches of all denominations. Christian radio and television programming feature confessed work, sex and shop "aholics." Christian bookstores are filled with books on addiction and recovery. Most of these apply the well known twelve step model to a whole host of assorted behaviors.

Our descent into calling sin sickness has brought us to the absurdity of defining any activity, involvement, or sensation a person finds consuming as a disease. Even good and worthy behavior, such as loving others, can be categorized as a disease. For example, Susan Peabody in *Addiction to Love* tells how she became interested in the subject of obsessive behavior in relationships. Her interest grew when she read Robin Norwood's book, *Women Who Love Too Much*. Peabody said the book helped her to recognize many of her own patterns of obsessive behavior (i.e., sin). Ready to make the appropriate changes in her life she began to look for a "Women Who Love Too Much" support group. Unfortunately, there were none in her area and so, using Norwood's book, she started her own meeting. Peabody wrote, "I became interested in teaching others about the 'disease' of 'loving too much'." Scripture warns us against the dangers of self-love, but never warns us of the harm of excessive love toward others.

The doctrine of sin is the unavoidable place one must begin in order to understand addictions. Sin is foundational to any consideration of human behavior. However, when every human problem is considered to be a disease or addiction, suggesting that sin may be the trouble is met with raised eyebrows and oftentimes sharp criticism. To bring sin into the discussion, even among evangelicals, is considered to be negative, insensitive and counter-productive. In a culture where self-esteem is something "we must have…and when it is unattainable everybody suffers"[6] talking about sin seems to be an attack on the psychological well-being of everyone. It is obvious to those who hold the disease-oriented perspective that those who question the disease model are confused or simply poorly informed.

Is the introduction of sin into the public discourse on depression, anxiety, addictions, etc. really negative, insensitive and counter-productive? Is it better for a person to hear God loves him and identifies with his pain rather than burdening him with more guilt by using the "s" word? Although we may not like to be reminded of it, we were all born in sin and sinning is what we do best. We enjoy sinning. We sin more than we think. We sin even when we would rather not sin (Romans 7:18, 19). It is difficult for some to concede, in a day so immersed in psychology, that personal sin is the root and cause of most of our day to day problems. Nevertheless, the reality that man sins and sin is the source of many of his problems is just stating a fact. To ignore the truth that there is something spiritually wrong with man, because it is believed it will harm his mental well-being or self-image, is to practice self-deception.

Today Christians do not rely on Scripture to shape their view of addictions and other sinful behaviors. While they admit the Bible does speak negatively about drunkenness, the prototype of all addictions, they insist alcoholism as a disease was not known in Bible times much like diabetes was not understood. So is addiction sin or sickness? What is the real problem of the addicted person?

Years ago, people believed that "alcoholism" was the result of the repeated sinful use of alcohol. Heavy drinking eventually led to addictive drinking. It was the same with drug users who eventually became addicts. Drunkards and addicts were therefore considered to be immoral and sinful. They were active agents, not passive, of their addictions. Today, the sin-model of addictions has been replaced by the sickness-model. Recent surveys have concluded approximately 80 percent of all Americans believe that alcoholism is a disease.

The core belief of the disease model of alcoholism is that alcoholics cannot control their drinking. They do not have the ability to drink moderately. Once they start drinking they will inevitably drink until they become intoxicated. At the same time alcoholism is seen as a progressive disease. This simply means it unalterably proceeds from its early stages to its ultimate true form. Stanton Peele, a psychologist, health-care researcher and leading figure in the addiction field, and Archie Brodsky, senior research associate at Harvard Medical School wrote:

> At first, it seems hard to understand what is meant by saying that something a person regularly does (such as drinking alcohol) is a disease. Habitual, voluntary behavior of this sort does not resemble what we normally think of as a disease, like cancer or diabetes. What is more, A.A., and even hospital programs for alcoholism, doesn't actually treat any biological causes of alcoholism.[7]

Peele and Brodsky go on to say that after decades of claiming to have discovered a biological connection of alcoholism, there is not one usable treatment. Hospitals for the past fifty years have been using the same old techniques (discussion groups and exhortations) they have always used. They continued:

Nor is there any biological method used to determine whether someone is an alcoholic other than by assessing how much that person drinks and the consequences of this drinking. And if we have no special biological information about treating or identifying alcoholism, we surely know nothing about the biological causes of "diseases" such as compulsive gambling, shopping, and loving, which have nothing to do with drugs or alcohol.[8]

Peele and Brodsky continue by reporting that these ideas and theories concerning alcoholism, when examined in the clear light of day, seem to be quite bizarre and contrary to common sense. The disease concept takes a set of precepts invented by a small group of severe, long-term drinkers back in the 1930's and applies them in an inappropriate way to people with a wide range of drinking and other problems.

The fact remains there is no identifiable biological or genetic mechanism to account for addictive behavior. However, if a gene were found to be the source of addiction to alcohol, would the same gene cause other addictions such as drugs, smoking, compulsive gambling and overeating? If so, everyone with these addictions would be genetically altered. Is there a gene for addiction to sex or addiction to lying? An individual without an addiction would be the notable exception.

How could an addiction like smoking be genetic? Why are some types of people more likely to smoke than others (about half of waitresses and car salesmen smoke, compared with about a tenth of lawyers and doctors)? And does believing that an addiction like smoking is genetic help the person quit (are all those smokers who quit not "genetically" addicted)? Returning to alcohol, are people really predestined biologically to become alcoholics and thus to become A.A. members? Think about the rock group Aerosmith: all five members of this group now belong to A.A., just as they once all drank and took drugs together. How unlikely a coincidence it is that five unrelated people with the alcoholic/addictive inheritance should run into one another and form a band![9]

The question is: If addiction isn't disease, then what is it? An addiction is a habitual response and a source of gratification or security. It is a way of coping with internal feelings and external pressures... [10]

The "hook", Peel and Brodsky go on to say, is that the behavior gives people a gratifying sensation they are not able to get any other way. The sensation is the payoff that keeps people coming back. It helps them forget their pain and discomfort. It distracts them from the overwhelming problems and difficulties of life and helps them to feel better.

The Bible has much to say about drunkenness. Drunkenness is never referred to as a sickness, but always as sin. For example, Noah planted a vineyard, drank of the wine and became drunk (Genesis 9:18-23). The consequence of his sin was shame. In his drunken state he did not cover himself, but lay naked exposing himself to his sons. Lot became drunk and committed incest with his daughters (Genesis 19:30-38). Men do things when they are intoxicated that would sicken and disgust them had they been sober. The sinfulness of drunkenness is clear in Paul's words to the Church when he wrote:

> But actually, I wrote to you not to associate with any so-called brother if he is an immoral person, or covetous, or an idolater, or a reviler, or a *drunkard*, or a swindler, even to eat with such a one (1 Corinthians 5:11, italics mine, NAS).

Paul continued:

> Or do you not know that the unrighteous will not inherit the kingdom of God? Do not be deceived; neither fornicators, nor idolaters, nor adulterers, nor effeminate, nor homosexuals, nor thieves, not the covetous, nor *drunkards*, not revilers, will inherit the kingdom of God (1 Corinthians 6:9-10, italics mine, NAS).

and

> Now the deeds of the flesh are evident, which are: immorality, impurity, sensuality, idolatry, sorcery, enmities, strife, jealousy, outbursts of anger, disputes, dissensions, factions, envying, *drunkenness*, carousing,

and things like these... (Galatians 5: 19-21, italics mine, NAS).

Solomon describes the irresistible appeal, cravings, irrationality and awful consequences of heavy drinking:

> Who has woe? Who has sorrow? Who has contentions? Who has complaining? Who has wounds without cause? Who has redness of eyes? Those who linger long over wine. Those who go to taste mixed wine. Do not look on the wine when it is red, when it sparkles in the cup, when it goes down smoothly; at the last it bites like a serpent and stings like a viper. Your eyes will see strange things and your mind will utter perverse things. And you will be like one who lies down in the middle of the sea, or like one who lies down on the top of a mast. They struck me, but I did not become ill; they beat me, but I did not know it. When shall I awake? I will seek another drink (Proverbs 23:29-35 NAS).

Paul emphasized the choice one makes when he wrote: "I *will* not be mastered by anything" (1 Corinthians 6:12, italics mine, NAS). Paul's emphasis is on the will. The continual willful use is what would finally bring a person under the power, so to speak, of a substance. Drunkenness is a lordship problem. It is a worship problem. It is a heart problem. Will God be your Master or will your desires rule over you? It boils down to the ancient command, "You shall have no other gods before Me." Addiction of any kind is the result of a person's willful sinful behavior.

A virus or bacteria, which people do not want to have, is very different from addiction. Addictions are a form of self-worship and are pursued by a person because they desire it (James1:14, 15). A drunkard drinks because of the benefit he receives from drinking. There is always a payoff. A person drinks for social reasons. His friends drink and he wants to be accepted by them and so he drinks. He drinks in order to forget his problems. Drinking temporarily alleviates the pain of a difficult situation or traumatic event. The desire to forget one's troubles or loneliness may be the reason for drinking. Pleasure is oftentimes the reason people drink. Others drink in order to relax. There is always a perceived reward. There is always a purpose to drinking. Self, not God and neighbor, is always the focus.

This does not mean that there is not a feeling of having been overcome by something outside of oneself like a virus. Addictions are mistaken for real diseases because there are certain similarities. A loss of control is a feeling one has when he has a disease. One feels powerless to invading bacteria. The problem lies when people stop using the word metaphorically and begin using it literally. They substitute the words "addiction is *like* a disease" for "addiction *is* a disease."

The Problem is Idolatry

The subject of idolatry is a dominate topic throughout the Bible. The first two commandments address the issue of idolatry:

> You shall have no other gods before Me (Exodus 20:3).

> You shall not make for yourself an idol, or any likeness of what is in heaven above or on the earth beneath or in the water under the earth. You shall not worship them or serve them; for I, the Lord your God, am a jealous God… (Exodus 20:4).

The declaration was against having gods other than Jehovah. Idolatry was not just a temporary or momentary danger to the Israelites or something they would overcome. Idolatry was a constant temptation and perpetual threat. It was a tendency they would never outgrow. The Old Testament books of Judges and Kings chronicle the repeated falling away of Israel into idolatry. Again and again we read of "high places" and "false gods." Again and again we read of captivities and chastisements as a result of idolatry. In the New Testament we read of the Apostles' expectations of the rise of idolatry in the Church:

> But actually, I wrote to you not to associate with any so-called brother if he is an immoral person, or covetous, or an idolater, or a reviler, or a drunkard, or a swindler…not to eat with such a one (1 Corinthians 5:11).

> Do not be idolaters, as some of them were (1 Corinthians 10:7).

> Therefore, my beloved, flee from idolatry (1 Corinthians 10:14).

Therefore consider the members of your earthly body as dead to immorality, impurity, passion, evil desire, and greed, which amount to idolatry (Colossians 3:5).

Little children, guard yourselves from idols (1 John 5:21).

The vulnerability toward idolatry lies deep in the human nature. Idolatry is natural and easily runs downhill. Spiritual worship runs against the grain of man's sinful nature and runs uphill. No one is safe from the dangers of idolatry. It is not an old-fashioned sin into which we will never likely fall. Those whom God has brought to Himself need to be reminded over and over again that He is Master. Jesus put it as plain as it can be put, "No man shall serve two masters." To depend on something other than God is a peril into which we are all liable to come. Pride makes a god of self. Covetousness makes a god of money. Sensuality makes a god out of the body. Whatever is esteemed, loved, feared, served, delighted in, and depended upon, more than God is made a god.

Idolatry best illustrates both the in-control and out-of-control experience of addiction. It is outside the boundaries of God when, in turning to idols, the individual seeks to find happiness, peace and contentment. Manipulating the idol for one's own benefit is the purpose of all idolatry. Idolaters do not want to be ruled by their idols. The idol is a means to an end. For example, the Bible says the prophets of Baal "leaped about the altar which they made" and "they cried with a loud voice and cut themselves" in order to manipulate Baal to do their will. Elyse Fitzpatrick wrote:

> "An integral part of false worship is learning how to get false gods to give us what we want. In essence, we make covenants with them, expecting them to bless us if we act in certain ways. It wasn't idolatrous for Rachel to desire children (Genesis 31, reference mine). No, she was idolatrous because her desire for children was the foremost desire in her heart. 'Give me children, or else I die!' is the cry of an idolater."[11]

It is not the goal of modern idolaters to be ruled by alcohol, drugs, love, people, food, sex, gambling, or work. The goal of the idolater is to get what he wants. His desire is for the substance or activity to give them good feelings, a sense of power, to help them forget their troubles or their past. Whatever his heart is craving is satisfied by the idol. Consequently, idolatry is and always has been rooted in the heart. The Prophet Ezekiel wrote, "Son of man, these men have set up their idols in their heart and have put right before their faces the stumbling block of their iniquity" (Ezekiel 14:3). Idolatry is a heart issue. From Adam and Eve's lust to be like God and eat that which was forbidden, to the inordinate craving and lust for love, food, sex and alcohol, mankind is guilty of idolatry.

When God created man He gave him certain desires and needs that, when kept in an appropriate context, would give him pleasure and joy. However, it is Satan's goal to exploit natural wants and desires so that the physical desires rule. Satan reverses God's order. Instead of people controlling their desires, their desires become idols that control them. They become enslaved, habituated and cannot say no.

Desires of the Heart Become Habits of Behavior

Do not store up for yourselves treasures on earth, where moth and rust destroy, and where thieves break in and steal. But store up for yourselves treasures in heaven, where neither moth nor rust destroys, and where thieves do not break in or steal; for where your treasure is, there your heart will be also. *treasure*

The eye is the lamp of the body; so then if your eye is clear, your whole body will be full of light. But if your eye is bad, your whole body will be full of darkness. *perspective* If then the light that is in you is darkness, how great is the darkness!

No one can serve two masters; for either he will hate the one and love the other, or he will be devoted to one and despise the other. You cannot serve God and wealth (Matthew 6:19-24) *serve*

One of the mistakes people make in interpreting the above passage is they think Jesus is exclusively referring to money. We must avoid interpreting this only with respect to money. 'Treasures' is a very large and all-inclusive term. It includes not only money, but also the things money can buy. However, Jesus is not so much concerned about possessions per se as He is concerned about one's attitude toward possessions, food, sex, etc. His warning is against worldly-mindedness; against getting satisfaction in this life from things that belong only to this world. We are all guilty of it, oftentimes without realizing it. Worldliness is so subtle it can infect even the most holy thing in life. Everyone has treasures or idols in some shape or form. Therefore, the command, "Do not store up for yourselves treasures on earth" is aimed at poor people as well as the rich.

Our Lord gives a very common sense argument against laying up treasures on earth. Treasures on earth do not last. Jesus said, "Do not store up for yourselves treasures on earth, where moth and rust destroy." There is an element of decay in earthly treasures. There is always something wrong with the things of this world. Idols never fully satisfy us. There is a tendency to get tired of these things. Although a man may appear to have everything he could desire, he still wants something more. That desire is why we are often talking about and seeking new things. Jesus continued, "And where thieves break in and steal." There are many thieves in this life that threaten and make us feel unsafe. Illness can steal health. A business loss can take life's savings. A company may collapse and leave many without jobs. Finally, death comes to steal life itself.

Worldliness has an effect on man's entire personality. Jesus said, "For where your treasure is, there your heart will be also." The heart is the first thing He mentions. Earthly things have an awful hold and power upon us. They grip our feelings, affections and all our sensibility. We love them. John wrote, "This is the judgment, that the Light has come into the world, and men loved the darkness rather than the Light, for their deeds were evil." We are absolutely gripped by these treasures.

Worldliness not only grips our heart, but it controls our thoughts. Our Lord said, "The eye is the lamp of the body; so then if your eye is clear, your whole body will be full of light. But if your eye is bad, your whole body will be full of darkness. If then the light that is in you is darkness, how great is the darkness!" (Matthew 6:23). Jesus uses the eye to illustrate the two ways we look at things in the world. First, the "clear eye" sees things as they truly are. The clear eye has single vision as opposed to double vision that distorts reality. Second is the "bad eye." The bad eye is characterized by blurry and double vision. The bad eye is tinted by certain prejudices, lusts and desires. Most people's thinking is based on these earthly treasures. Many of the beliefs and ideologies people hold are controlled entirely by prejudices and desires; not by clear or pure thinking.

Finally, treasures affect man's will. Jesus said, "No one can serve two masters; for either he will hate the one and love the other, or he will be devoted to one and despise the other. You cannot serve God and wealth." As soon as one mentions the word serve, one is talking about the will, man's actions. Our behavior is logically preceded by our thinking. In other words, the exercise of will is determined by thinking. Thinking is determined by the heart. Therefore, earthly treasures have a very powerful influence upon the whole man. Treasures seize hold of the heart, mind and will. Ultimately they affect and determine our relationship with God. This is an obvious truth. "No one can serve two masters; for either he will hate the one and love the other, or he will be devoted to one and despise the other. You cannot serve God and wealth." Worldly things make a totalitarian and tyrannical demand on our lives. They command all of our love. It is "either/or;" there is no compromise. They want all our devotion. They expect us to live exclusively for them...but so does God.

Why does Jesus warn us about these things? Why are His instructions concerning storing up treasures on earth so necessary? Why do the apostles warn us of these things? There can be only one answer. It is because of the horrific effects of sin. His words tell us a great deal about sin and what sin has done to mankind.

Sin is obviously something that has had an alarming and disconcerting effect upon the normal functioning of man. Man's terrible predicament is that he is no longer governed by his highest faculties (pre-Fall), but by something else. He is controlled by something secondary, inferior and substandard to the purpose for which God created him. He is controlled by his desires, his affections and his lusts. That is the effect of sin.

Our failure to recognize these things is the trouble with the world today in calling sin sickness. One can be mastered, bound or enslaved to any sinful behavior, attitude or thought. Scripture constantly warns us of the danger of becoming habituated to sin of all kinds.

Knowing this, that our old self was crucified with Him, in order that our body of sin might be done away with, so that we would no longer be *slaves* to sin (Romans 6:6, italics mine).

Therefore do not let sin *reign* in your mortal body so that you obey its lusts (Romans 6:12, italics mine).

And do not *go on presenting* the members of your body to sin... (Romans 6:13, italics mine).

For sin shall not be *master* over you... (Romans 6:14, italics mine).

For we also once were foolish ourselves, disobedient, deceived, *enslaved* to various lusts and pleasures... (Titus 3: 3, italics mine).

For everyone who partakes only of milk is *accustomed* to the word of righteousness, for he is an infant. But solid food is for the mature, who because of *practice* have their senses *trained* to discern good and evil (Hebrews 5:13-14, italics mine)

Not forsaking our own assembling together, as is the *habit* of some, but encouraging one another; and all the more as you see the day drawing near (Hebrews 10:25, italics mine).

Therefore, since we have so great a cloud of witnesses surrounding us, let us also lay aside every encumbrance and the sin which so easily *entangles* us, and let us run with endurance the race that is set before us... (Hebrews 12:1, italics mine).

God made man with the capacity to formulate habits. If man did not have this ability, he would have to think about *everything* he does or says. Every action would have to be thought out and performed in a methodical, meticulous, and laborious way. The ability to create habits allows people to carry out complicated tasks comfortably and automatically. Habit allows a person to write a letter to a friend without having to relearn how to write the letters of the alphabet. Habit allows people to walk, talk, and do thousands of different things and combinations of things without thinking about every detail.

Over time, and by practice, people become habituated to certain tasks. The writer of Hebrews wrote about habits when he said, "But solid food is for the mature, who because of *practice* have their senses *trained* to discern good and evil" (Hebrews 5:14, italics mine). People become habituated to many behaviors and attitudes. For example, greed is a learned behavior or habit. Peter wrote, "Having eyes full of adultery and that never cease from sin, enticing unstable souls, having a heart *trained* in greed, accursed children" (2 Peter 2:14, italics mine). Some people are never satisfied or content. Paul was one of those people, but he said he learned how to be content. He wrote, "Not that I speak from want; for I have *learned* to be content in whatever circumstances I am" (Philippians 4:11). People who have sinful habits can change. Jeremiah wrote, "You also can do good who are *accustomed* to doing evil" (Jeremiah 13:23). Paul wrote to Titus concerning believers who had been enslaved or habituated to sinful practices, but had changed. He said, "For we also once *were* foolish ourselves, disobedient, deceived, *enslaved* to various lusts and pleasures, spending our life in malice and envy, hateful, hating one another" (Titus 3:3, italics mine). When Paul wrote to the Corinthian believers, he reminded some of them about their past sinful practices which they had successfully put off. He wrote:

> Or do you not know that the unrighteous shall not inherit the kingdom of God? Do not be deceived; neither fornicators, nor idolaters, nor adulterers, nor effeminate, nor homosexuals, nor thieves, nor {the} covetous, nor drunkards, nor revilers, nor swindlers, shall inherit the kingdom of God. And such were some of you; but you were washed, but you were sanctified, but you were justified in the name of the Lord Jesus Christ, and in the Spirit of our God (1 Corinthians 6:9-11).

While habit, a blessing from God, makes life easier and more comfortable, habit can also be a curse. Sinful habits are the source of many of people's problems. People become habituated to sinful behaviors and attitudes. Sanctification involves helping believers put off sinful habits and put on the Biblical alternative habits. It is putting off the deeds of the flesh and putting on the fruit of the Spirit (Galatians 5). Habits are learned ways of living, and therefore can be unlearned and replaced. Habits are formed when something is done repeatedly. Over time it becomes habitual.

The gradual descent into idolatry begins somewhat innocently until eventually the idol serves more and more purposes in a person's life. It takes a focal point or center stage and becomes the axis of everyday living. The tendency of our psychologized culture is to talk about the uncontrollable characteristic of "addiction." People talk about the external thing controlling them. The Bible brings in the crucial element of the heart. The heart controls man. Man is responsible. We desire and pursue the behavior or substance. The tantalizing call to sin is rooted in the heart, and as it is practiced over a period of time becomes a habit. That is the fundamental nature of sin. All people sin, all people sin differently, all people sin habitually. What psychology calls addictive behavior (the disease model), the Bible calls habitual sinful behavior. The addict is said to be sick and his disease is theorized to have a biological or genetic cause. However, in the sin model the heart is the center of behavior. The heart, which is biased against God and for self, is the source of the problem. It is not an outside force that has invaded one's body; it is one's own desire. The problem is not God or the circumstances; it is the individual himself. Lust, not biology or genetics, is the principle problem.

James demonstrates the progression from temptation to sin and how this leads to habitual behavior, writing:

> But each one is tempted when he is carried away and enticed by his own lust. Then when lust has conceived, it gives birth to sin; and when sin is accomplished, it brings forth death (1:14-15).

The process of sin begins with an event that stirs a desire within a person. By allowing the situation to stir an inner desire the individual creates the temptation. Thus, God does not tempt. James said, "But each one is tempted when he is carried away and enticed by his *own* lust." At this point the temptation can be cut short by changing one's behavior (Philippians 4:8). For example, if the temptation is a beautiful woman at the mall, a man may turn and begin talking to his wife. He may walk to a different area of the store where the woman is no longer visible. The emphasis is on changing thoughts by changing behavior. If he does not change his behavior and allows himself to contemplate carrying out the sin, it will lead to adultery in the heart. Again James wrote, "Then when lust has *conceived*." James uses the analogy of a woman giving birth to show how temptation evolves into outward sin. Conception, or sin of the heart, occurs on the inside. This stage can be cut short by repenting of the inner sin (sin in the heart) and changing behavior. However, if one allows oneself to continue, it will lead to an outward act of sin. James wrote, "It gives birth to sin."

Thus, sin has manifested itself in an outward action.

The inner consideration of an improper desire will lead, in time, to the conception and birth of an outward act of sin. Left unchecked, an outer act of sin will become a continuous practice of a person's life.[12] Paul warns, "Therefore do not let sin reign in your mortal body so that you obey its lust" (Romans 6:12). Paul said he had to "discipline his body and make it his slave," as opposed to being a slave to the desires of his body (1 Corinthians 9:27).

Sin is Our Only Hope

To abandon sin is to abandon hope. Sin is the pivot or hinge on which hope turns. Modern statements regarding sin will prove how often we are more sympathetic with psychological explanations than with Biblical ones. To deviate, even the smallest amount, from the truth of sin will lead to wrong thinking and a loss of hope. Once settled regarding the doctrine of sin, good reasoning and hope follow.

One would think calling sin sickness is so obviously contrary to Scripture that evangelicals everywhere would rise up and expose the error. Unfortunately, the disease-model has squeezed out the sin-model not only in the minds of unbelievers, but believers. The consequence has had a devastating effect on evangelism and sanctification. People with problems of living, Christian and non-Christian, seeking help from the Church or a Christian agency are likely to be told their problem is a psychological disorder or illness. They will be referred to a psychiatrist or psychologist and/or will be encouraged to attend a Church-based recovery program that is touted to be "Christ-centered." The person is well on the way to being a patient in much the same way as if he had pneumonia or a broken leg.

The sickness model of behavior has a defeating and disheartening effect in people's lives. Many people fail to understand when a psychiatrist or psychologist makes what is believed to be a medical diagnosis, it is in reality only the identification of observable behavior or experience. Consider, for example, how diseases are diagnosed in comparison to how psychological problems are diagnosed. A patient complains of certain symptoms. His physician suspects a particular disease. However, before the doctor gives a definitive diagnosis he performs several objective tests (x-ray, blood test, MRI, etc.). The tests will confirm or repudiate his suspicions. The physician does not make a diagnosis based solely on his patient's symptoms or complaint, but on verifiable evidence concerning both the cause and nature of the problem.

Contrary to what many people believe, this is not how psychological problems are diagnosed. A psychologist assumes because a person has certain feelings, thoughts or behaviors over a prescribed period of time, he has a psychological problem. This is assumed even though the cause has not been proven, nor can it be, by scientific methods. The problem lies in the foundations of psychological theories. These foundations are simply not adaptable to scientific examination. Nevertheless, the decision is uncritically accepted as an incontestable and unquestionable diagnosis. The diagnosis may sound plausible, but it never moves beyond the subjective into the realm of objective truth. This is true generally speaking of the historical psychologies, as well as biological psychiatry which dominates counseling today. Biological psychiatrists seek to explain life through an interpretation that excludes God, sin, Christ and sanctification. In turn, people begin to think that the primary solution to their problem is not spiritual, but physical or materialistic in nature. When it comes to responsibility for actions, the biopsychiatrist says YOU are not really you. You are just a body and a body part has malfunctioned. You can be fixed from the *outside* by a drug. The psychologist attributes your unpleasant emotions and bad behavior to a painful past, low self-esteem, or an empty love tank. The solution to your problem is "talking treatment."

A notorious component of sin is the loss of man's sense of responsibility. Adam and Eve ran, hid, covered up and shifted the blame. Adam said, "The woman whom You gave to be with me, she gave me from the tree, and I ate." Eve said, "The serpent deceived me, and I ate" (Genesis 3:12, 13). Psychology, with satanic shrewdness, destroys a person's capacity to know and feel he has sinned. It figuratively and literally drugs man to where he feels no guilt or responsibility. It numbs the conscience, dulling the voice of the Holy Spirit in the life of a Christian. It feeds our natural bias toward self-exaltation. It makes us feel we are sick when we are perfectly well. And by the ingenious trickery of our own heart, we boast that our blindness is true sight and *we are ourselves* absolutely fit to meet our moral and spiritual needs. The reasoning is that since man understands man, we logically should go to man for the solution. All this is accomplished by Satan's old, but proven scheme of usurping God's truth and promising to man god-likeness and superior knowledge. However, only in the confession "I have sinned" can hope be found:

> "If we say that we have no sin, we are deceiving ourselves and the truth is not in us. If we confess our sins, He is faithful and righteous to forgive us our sins and to cleanse us from all unrighteousness. If we say that we have not sinned, we make Him a liar and His word is not in us" (1 John 18-10).

"God is Light, and in Him there is no darkness at all" (1 John 1:5) and consequently God cannot have fellowship with darkness. The nature of light is to illuminate and to make things known. God is Light and therefore, all things are known by Him. God is Light and therefore He is truth. God cannot speak falsehood. Man devises and concocts things that are not true for his own purpose. God creates irrefutable facts. We see things as they *appear* to be. God, who is Light, sees things *as they exist*. God never misrepresents. Light illuminates what *is*. Man is always rushing around with his paint and glitter trying to make things appear to be equal to the precious and valued. Man works hard to make the imitation look like the real thing. All this is contrary to the way of the Lord. Is 55

The natural tendency of the sinful heart is to try to be what it is not. The love of praise compels us to pretend we are better than we are. Fear of condemnation and reproof is an equally powerful means of producing hypocrisy. We must by all means strive against psychological thinking that tells us we have not sinned when God clearly tells us we have. To say rebelliousness, drunkenness, lying, stealing, fornication, etc. is not sin when God clearly calls it such is a fearful delusion that must be put off. Pretending the deeds of the flesh (Galatians 5:19-21) are diseases makes God a liar. To attempt to defend these ideas is abominable. To embrace them, by implication or innuendo, is contemptuous. To cling to such a lie is to call light darkness and darkness light. One may say he has fellowship with God, but the facts do not correspond with the words.

Realizing something is wrong is the first step toward setting it right again. Jesus said the prodigal son "came to himself." It was the turning point in his relationship with his father. Had he never realized his true condition, he would have remained a prodigal. His life would have been a warning to all instead of encouragement and instruction. His confession, "Father, I have sinned" led to a precious reception described by Luke: "So he got up and came to his father. But while he was still a long way off, his father saw him and felt compassion for him, and *ran* and embraced him and kissed him" (15:20, italics mine). Under a burden of shame, the prodigal son came slowly and fearfully toward his father's house. By contrast, when his father saw him he ran to meet him, and while others loathed touching him for he had just come from feeding swine, the compassion of a loving father greets him with arms of mercy and overwhelms him with affection.

The parable teaches us that true penitents are dear to God and welcomed by the Lord Jesus Christ. However, there is no such reception when one has been deceived and is convinced he is sick when he is sinful. Where there is no sensibility toward sin, there is no repentance of it and no forgiveness granted. There is no help for those who admit no need for help. Our Lord's words to the Pharisees who murmured against Him were fitting and in perfect order. Jesus said, "It is not those who are healthy who need a physician, but those who are sick."

Those who are not sick do not need a physician. A legitimate physician does not prescribe medication, nor does a surgeon perform surgery on a person who is perfectly well. To go to the doctor's office to tell him you are perfectly fine and you have never felt better in your life is silly. In the same way, if we think we are morally fine though physically sick, we will not repent. If our bad behavior is a disease, we will not go to Christ for cleansing. If, on the other hand, we decide to call sin sin, we have made a major shift in our perception of reality. We have acknowledged, as the prodigal son, that something is wrong with our self. The confession requires responsibility on our part. Had the son shifted blame to his circumstances or attributed his anxiety to a condition other than sin, he would have spiraled deeper and deeper, as do so many today, into depression and despair. Repentance and being absolved of his sin reversed the spiral of gloom and despondency.

A physician should be where there are sick people who need his service. It was obvious the Pharisees felt themselves morally whole, as do those who attribute their sinful behavior to illness. People who call sin a disease and treat it as such with talk therapy and/or medication become mired in an endless cycle of more talking and more chemical manipulation of feelings and thoughts. There is no hope; there is no cure. In his book, *Diseasing of America,* Stanton Peele wrote:

> People's belief that they have a disease makes it less likely that they will outgrow the problem. For this reason, disease approaches are most inappropriate and dangerous for the young. Treatment programs for chemical dependence stress to young substance abusers that they will *always* have a drug-taking or drinking problem. This almost *guarantees* that relapses will be frequent, when under ordinary conditions the vast majority would outgrow their youthful excesses. Treatment thus serves mainly as an impediment to the normal process of "maturing out" of addiction.[13]

Sin is our only hope. When sin is substituted for sickness the emphasis is on diagnosing instead of judgment or rebuke. Treatment is the focus instead of repentance, forgiveness and biblical change. To cherish the illusion that sin is sickness is to forfeit forgiveness and restoration of fellowship with God. For the Christian, sanctification is thwarted; for the unbeliever, eternal damnation.

Notes
1. Barbara Brown Taylor, *Speaking of Sin, The Lost Language of Salvation,* (Cambridge, MA: Cowley Publications, 2000), p. 5.
2. Henri Blocher, *Original Sin, Illuminating the Riddle,* (Grand Rapids, MI: William B. Eerdmans Publishing Company, 1997), p. 105.
3. Howard J. Clinebell, Jr., *Mental Health Through Christian Community* (New York, NY: Abington Press, 1972), p. 27.
4. Oswald Chambers, *Biblical Ethics The Moral Foundations of Life with The Philosophy of Sin,* (Grand Rapids, MI: Discovery House Publishers, 1998), p. 127.
5. Stanton Peele and Archie Brodsky, *The Truth About Addiction and Recovery,* (New York, NY: Fireside, 1991), p. 26.
6. James Dobson, *Hide and Seek* (Grand Rapids, MI: Fleming H. Revell, 1971), 21.
7. Stanton Peele and Archie Brodsky, *The Truth About Addiction and Recovery,* (New York, NY: Fireside, 1991), p. 23.
8. *Ibid.,* p. 24.
9. *Ibid.,* p. 27.
10. *Ibid.,* p. 42.
11. Elyse Fitzpatrick, *Idols Of the Heart ,* (Phillipsburg, PA: P&R Publishing, 2001), p. 24.

12. For a detailed exposition of James 1:13-15 on the stages of temptation, read Jay Adams' book, *A Thirst for Wholeness.*

13. Stanton Peele, *Diseasing of America,* (San Francisco, CA: Jossey-Bass Publishers, 1989), p. 27.

Chapter Three
~~Sin~~ Sickness in the Camp

I did not know when I first became a Christian that the development of my understanding of the meaning and implications of my Christian faith would eventually lead me to a crossroads where I would have to choose between two masters–between the mental health professionals and Christianity, between the mental health religion and Jesus Christ. But this is what has occurred, and I have made my choice.

Seth Farber, *Unholy Madness,
The Church's Surrender to Psychiatry*[1]

Scripture says the early Christians "turned the world upside down" (Acts 17:6KJV). In our generation the world is turning the Church upside down.

John MacArthur, Jr. *Ashamed of the Gospel*[2]

O Timothy, guard what has been entrusted to you, avoiding worldly and empty chatter and the opposing arguments of what is falsely called knowledge which some have professed and thus gone astray from the faith.

Apostle Paul, *1 Timothy 6:20, 21*

A Trojan Horse

Over three thousand years ago the Trojan War was fought and won by the Greek army. However, their victory was not the most significant feature about the war. What was significant was *how* they conquered the city. Troy, like most cities of that time, was surrounded by protective walls. To fool the people of Troy, the Greeks built a wooden horse and presented it to them as a gift. The inhabitants of Troy had no idea the *gift* would soon lead to ruin. Hiding inside the horse were Greek soldiers. During the night, the soldiers came out of the horse and let the Greek army into the city. They plundered, looted and burned the city of Troy. The people of Troy had unwittingly invited an enemy into their city and it destroyed them.

Evangelicalism has opened its gates to a Trojan horse. This horse is not a literal wooden horse filled with enemy soldiers, but is the teachings of modern psychology. The integration of modern psychology with the Bible is indeed one of the most challenging issues facing the Church today. Some Christian psychologists have become so beloved that to criticize them would be almost like criticizing the Bible itself. While their intentions may be good, intentions are not the issue. The issue is whether today's Christians are mixing men's ideas with the Bible. Amazingly, most Christian leaders today who rightly cry so fervently against false teachings are saying little if anything about subtle shifts in biblical interpretation that undermine the faith of millions. In many cases it reflects a lack of awareness and understanding of the teachings of psychology.

It is hard to evangelize people and talk with them about their sin when the line between sin and sickness is so vague. It is a mournful spectacle indeed to see a man refuse the mercy of God because he has learned that his anger is due to a "sickness" called oppositional defiant disorder. There are many people in recovery, but sinners are becoming more and more difficult to find. Could this be the reason why the "seeker friendly story" has in many places replaced, as the hymn goes, the old old story? When Christians themselves are challenging the legitimacy of their sin, are we surprised when unbelievers deny theirs? Is stealing sin? Are anger, fornication, drunkenness, and selfishness sin? The answer evangelicalism seems to give is yes and no.

There has never been a time when Christianity has not been threatened by false doctrines and worldliness. The past century has not been any different. The evangelical movement has been one long, continuous struggle against errant liberal theology and worldly compromise. In the last 200 years we have seen the emergence of one of the compromises...modernism, and then its successor, postmodernism.

Modernism to Postmodernism

While people have always committed sins, they at least acknowledged these were sins. A century ago

> *a person may have committed adultery flagrantly
> and in defiance of God and man, but he would have
> admitted that what he was doing was a sin. What we
> have today is not only immoral behavior, but a loss of
> moral criteria. This is true even in the Church. We face
> not only a moral collapse but a collapse of meaning.*[3]

Gene Edward Veith, Jr.

Modernism is a movement of thought that can be traced to the period in European history known as the Enlightenment. Advances in science, such as Isaac Newton's findings confirming the laws of gravity, signaled that human inquiry into nature could be made independent from Scripture. People became modern and were "enlightened" in their thinking. This set into motion a search for other laws that not only governed every aspect of nature, but also society, government, human relationships and even man's mind. The universe, life and man himself were reduced to mere mechanism, fully explainable and predictable.

Then in 1859, Charles Darwin published his book, *Origin of Species*. At the time, many Christians thought Darwin's view was just another passing fad. Decades later, the notion of a natural world, with no place for God, has reshaped every academic discipline. In the same way the natural world had moved forward through the stages of evolution, it was thought human society would also progress into a brighter future. This optimism toward man's reason and science has profoundly shaped the fields of psychology and psychiatry. Both are thoroughly saturated with evolutionary thinking. It is assumed man is merely an evolved animal and his behavior problems are evaluated on an animalistic basis. Experiments with rats, monkeys and other animals, even insects, are used for guidance in dealing with human problems. Humans are viewed as part of the great big machine of nature. It was once thought people made moral choices, but now behavior is attributed to genetic coding or chemical reactions. Human behavior, selflessness and selfishness, kindness and cruelty, love and hate, have all been turned into a strictly biological science. By far the most serious indictment is evolution's destructive effects upon Christian theology; the nature of man and his behavior.

Postmodernism has also been a powerful influence in our culture and the Church. Of course, this does not mean modernism has completely disappeared. Regarding counseling, postmodern eclecticism (borrowing from a variety of world views) and pragmatism (doing whatever works) are common ways of thinking.

Like modernists, postmodernists believe man is no different than the rest of nature. However, postmodernism and modernism differ in some very significant areas. Modernists see people as gears in a huge *material* machine. Postmodernists see people as gears in a *social* machine. Modernists see people as they are affected by the processes of nature and biology. Postmodernists see social processes, especially language, as having a primary effect on people. Postmodernists emphasize the effects language has in shaping people's thinking. People think in words and communicate in words. People's perception and ideas are what connects them to reality and provides meaning. Culture and society creates meaning. In his book, *The Death of Truth*, Dennis McCallum wrote:

> If we say, for example, "the room is hot," we consciously substitute perception for reality, subjectivity for objectivity. We should say, "the room *appears* to be hot," or "I perceive it to be hot." Instead, by stating perceptions as though they are reality, our words actually insulate us from reality. We confuse the symbol...words...with reality. We think we understand something because we have formed a word for it. As cultures accept definitions for words, they solidify the confusion between symbol and the real.[4]

The postmodern idea that culture creates reality through the definitions of words has had a significant impact and has contributed to the acceptance of the psychological labeling of sin as sickness. Subjectivity is substituted for objectivity. Definitions of what is normal or abnormal, sin or sickness, reside not in objective tests that discover pathology (x-ray, blood test, urinalysis, MRI), but are cultural definitions placed on behavior and given names. In other times or places the behavior may have been considered normal, rational or reasonable. For example, it has only been relatively recently that sinful behavior like fornication or stealing has been considered to be an addiction. Only recently has love been categorized as a disease. In the past, homosexuality was considered abnormal, and in some cultures it still is. Depending on the culture and historical setting, behaviors now regarded as disease were considered immoral and sinful. Today, those ideas are viewed as being intolerant, narrow-minded, old-fashioned, and uninformed.

Classifying Disease

Fundamental to understanding the world around us is the ability to identify and classify things. We classify solids, liquids, stones, money and masterpieces. We assert some things belong to class A, and other things are non-A. If, for some reason, society adopts a new criteria of classification and transfers all non-A's into A, then A would encompass all things and the classification would be useless. The usefulness of any method of classification and its respective names depends on the fact that it includes some things and excludes others. This is exactly what has happened in medicine and psychiatry for the past century. In the beginning there were explicit and distinct maladies such as cancer, syphilis, strokes, polio, fractures and other injuries. A class was created for "diseases." The class was limited to members that shared a common characteristic toward anatomic or physiologic pathology. As time went on, behaviors like gambling, drunkenness, selfishness, rebelliousness, love and countless others were added to this class. They were added not because they were discovered to be bodily diseases, but because the *criterion* of what was considered a disease was changed.

The Church has accepted the new criterion of classifying disease without question. Sin is now sickness. There may be a variety of symptoms of a disease, like shortness of breath, but the symptom is not the disease. Behavior may cause disease—for example, smoking may cause cancer, and drinking alcohol may cause cirrhosis of the liver, but the behavior is not the disease. Behavior may be the consequence of disease. A brain tumor or Alzheimer's Disease may affect a person's behavior, but the behavior itself is not the disease.

Today people do not have a clear idea of what is and what is not a disease. It is not surprising since the term is used to describe a multitude of not only physiological problems, but also emotions, experiences and behaviors. If we are going to be able to use the term with precision, the word must have a limited meaning. It is necessary to be able to clearly distinguish between literal and metaphorical uses. Everyone would agree that a virus causes disease, but a computer virus causes no physical illness. No one confuses computer viruses with biological agents. Typhoid fever is a disease, but spring fever, cabin fever or love-sickness is not. However, used in an abstract or theoretical sense some may argue spring fever, cabin fever and love sickness are diseases. The same could be said of the "holiday blues."

There is no uniformity in thought as to whether spring fever, cabin fever or the holiday blues are diseases. This is why there are such futile discussions about whether addiction, anxiety, antisocial behavior, depression, loving too much, gambling and so on are diseases. The terms lack specific meaning; therefore, we cannot know what literal disease is and what counts as metaphorical disease. The attempt to discover organic disease under the constraints of fixed criteria and the requirements of empirical evidence will not lead to such confusion. However, when psychiatry is unconstrained by fixed criteria and empirical evidence, it will always conclude any phenomenon studied by an observer may be defined as a disease. This serves the purpose of psychiatry. More diseases equal more patients. More patients mean greater financial rewards.

Using Words to Rebel Against God

Postmodern theorists assume language is a human construct. Christians could not disagree more. Language existed before man or the universe was created:

> In the beginning was the Word, and the Word was with God, and the Word was God. He was in the beginning with God. All things came into being through Him, and apart from Him nothing came into being that has come into being. In Him was life, and the life was the Light of men. The Light shines in the darkness, and the darkness did not comprehend it. And the Word became flesh, and dwelt among us, and we saw His glory, glory as of the only begotten from the Father, full of grace and truth (John 1:1-5, 14).

Creation was accomplished *ex nihilo* merely by the spoken word of the Creator. "Then God said, 'Let there be light'; and there was light" (Genesis 1:3) and so on. God spoke into existence what He willed. "By the word of the Lord the heavens were made... For He spoke, and it was done" (Psalm 33:6, 9). Everything in the universe from the great scientific laws, the language code of DNA and the mathematical precision of physics has their origin in the Word of God.

Man was made in the image of his Creator. God's image in man required a means of communication between God and man and also between man and man. God spoke and Adam spoke. Using the remarkable phenomenon of language Adam conversed with God and Eve; and was able to examine and name all the animals:

> Out of the ground the Lord God formed every beast of the field and every bird of the sky, and brought them to the man to see what he would call them; and whatever the man called a living creature, that was its name. The man gave names to all the cattle, and to the birds of the sky, and to every beast of the field, but for Adam there was not found a helper suitable for him (Genesis 2:19, 20).

As the animals passed before Adam he gave each one a quick appraisal and an appropriate name. "Whatever the man called a living creature that was its name." God allowed Adam to make up his own words for the creatures God had made. God has His words and now man has his words.

Man's words are different from God's words. God is infallible and so are His words. Man's words are not sacred words, but are temporary, impermanent and random. The dissimilarity between God's words and man's is all the more obvious in the account of the Fall. Satan spoke and for the first time there were words contrary to God's words. Satan used words to seduce Adam and Eve. Language became corrupted. Adam and Eve used language to rationalize, criticize and shift the blame. Adam said, "The woman whom You gave to be with me, she gave me from the tree, and I ate" (Genesis 3:12). Eve retorted, "The serpent deceived me, and I ate" (Genesis 3: 13).

Another example of how man has used language to rise up against God is found in the story of the Tower of Babel:

> Now the whole earth used the same language and the same words. It came about as they journeyed east, that they found a plain in the land of Shinar and settled there. They said to one another, 'Come, let us make bricks and burn them thoroughly.' And they used brick for stone, and they used tar for mortar. They said, 'Come, let us build for ourselves a city, and a tower whose top will reach into heaven, and let us make for ourselves a name, otherwise we will be scattered abroad over the face of the whole earth' (Genesis 11:1-4).

God's instructions to man following the flood were for man to be fruitful and populate the earth (Genesis 9:1). As the people migrated eastward from the region of Ararat, they came to the fertile plains of Mesopotamia where they decided to settle. It was there in the land of Shinar that Nimrod led a rebellion against God. He called a council and made an official declaration to build a city with a great tower reaching to the heavens. It would be a carefully planned urban development designed for permanence. It would be a self-sufficient society no longer dependent upon God. This would be their home. They were not concerned with God's plans for they said, "let us make for *ourselves* a name." They clearly acknowledged their purpose was in opposition to God's command when they declared, "Come let us build... otherwise we will be scattered abroad over the face of the whole earth." God's purpose had become so endangered that as in the days of Noah, divine intervention became necessary.

God saw the problem in the unity of the people. A common language made it possible for them to cooperate, organize, formulate and implement their plans. God could no longer ignore their rebellion, so He confused their language:

> The Lord came down to see the city and the tower which the sons of men had built. The Lord said, 'Behold, they are one people, and they all have the same language. And this is what they began to do, and now nothing which they purpose to do will be impossible for them. Come, let us go down and there confuse their language, so that they will not understand one another's speech. So the Lord scattered them abroad from there over the face of the whole earth; and they stopped building the city. Therefore its name was called Babel, because there the Lord confused the language of the whole earth; and from there the Lord scattered them abroad over the face of the whole earth' (Genesis 11:5-9).

Human language after Babel became confused. It has become difficult to understand one another. Although we presume to erect large and magnificent structures with our language, the truth is we still use our words to rebel against God's Word. Such is the case when we call sin sickness.

The Axe is Laid at the Root

If a person is to have a correct view of the Christian faith, he must understand the vital subject of sin. To make a mistake here would be very harmful. <u>Wrong views about Christianity are generally traceable</u> <u>to wrong views about man and sin.</u> Words like justification and sanctification are just "words" that, without sin, convey no meaning. "Christ died for our sins" (1 Corinthians 15:3), if sin is not perceived to be the problem, is just viewed to be another religious cliché. <u>Sin is the</u> <u>core issue on which the Church is commissioned to speak.</u> We can no more have a gospel without sin than we can have a gospel without Jesus Christ. To evade sin and responsibility is not new, but it is dangerous. By suggesting there is another explanation for troubles and difficulties, the devil deludes us and sabotages the gospel.

The medical model of sin is dangerous because it damns people. It undercuts social morality. In a day of high crime and antisocial behavior, calling sin sickness undermines the individual's responsibility to control his behavior. <u>The disease model actually inflames behaviors.</u> <u>It legitimizes, reinforces and excuses sinful behaviors and attitudes in</u> <u>believers and unbelievers alike.</u> Christians who embrace this worldly view <u>put aside their armor.</u> They become <u>vulnerable,</u> not only to temptation, but also to <u>deception</u> and <u>weakness.</u> <u>Resisting sin is difficult</u> <u>when it is relabeled disease.</u> It opens believers up to becoming enslaved to sin. It disrupts the process of sanctification. <u>Churches are filled with</u> <u>Christians who are convinced they are sick instead of sinful.</u> <u>They are</u> <u>convinced that Prozac is the answer to their problems and do not even</u> <u>entertain a thought about repentance.</u>

The moral tone of our society has been directly due to the loss of the <u>authority</u> of the Bible and the belief in the <u>sufficiency</u> of Scripture. The teachings of Christ and the apostles have been replaced with the teachings of Sigmund Freud, Carl Rogers, Abraham Maslow and many more. Sin is suppressed and falsely called sickness. While we may be alarmed at the decline of morality inside and outside of the Church, we are denying the very doctrine useful in dealing with it. We pray for revival, but there is <u>no humility</u> among believers and <u>no confession of sin.</u> This is consistent with what people are told about their problems and difficulties. <u>There</u> <u>will never be urgency for revival if the problem is biological rather than</u> <u>spiritual.</u> By calling sin sickness we shoot ourself in the foot.

John the Baptist said, "Indeed the axe is already laid at the root of the trees" (Luke 3:9). A new order has come. The main point of difference is this: <u>the gospel of Jesus Christ does not deal superficially, but goes to</u> <u>the very root of man's problem.</u> There is no mere ruffling of leaves and shaking branches; <u>the axe is laid at the root of the tree.</u> The gospel is plain and clear. Sin is sin and all have sinned. Mankind is under the wrath of God. Christ died a vicarious death, the just for the unjust. People must repent of their sins or they will perish. The forerunner, the great herald, of the Christian gospel did not make indefinite or imprecise statements. No ambiguous or foggy words came from his lips.

The tendency today is to forget the roots. Ignore the essentials. The doctrine of sin is understandably disliked by the world. Moreover, what is alarming and tragic is the opposition Christians have for the doctrine of sin. There was a time when sin was clear and definite. But who can say that is true today? Vagueness characterizes what we think of sin. Sin is sin, but it is sickness too. We are not really sure. We must consult the "experts" who are trained in detecting these things. There is no clarity of view, no definition of position, our language is confused. In fact, any attempt to recognize a clear distinction between sin and sickness is branded as being anti-Christian and unloving. The apparent glory of Christianity today is in its vagueness. Satan glories in the Church's preparedness to say man is sinful and at the same time not sinful, but sick.

David wrote, "Tremble and do not sin" (Psalm 4:4). While there is considerable trembling due to anxiety, fear, drugs and alcohol, there is not much trembling about sin. Trembling on account of sin is an emotion one does not hear much about, even in Church. This is a flippant age. People are triflers rather than tremblers. If there is a doctrine which has unusual seriousness and gravity to it, as sin does, man reduces it down to something with less grave consequences. Sickness is bad enough, but sin is worse. David continues, "Offer the sacrifices of righteousness" (Psalm 4:5). When the people of David's day brought a sacrifice, they would lay their hand on the victim and make confession of sin. They would confess their pride, unbelief, lying, anger, bitterness, disobedience and drunkenness. They would own up to their transgressions. Today people confess they are alcoholics, codependents, addicts and so on. No one is admitting they have sinned.

Notes

1. Seth Farber, Unholy Madness, *The Church's Surrender to Psychiatry*, (Downers Grove, IL: InterVarsity Press, 1999), p. 11,12.
2. John MacArthur, *Ashamed of the Gospel*, (Wheaton, IL: Crossway Books, 1993), p. 51.
3. Gene Edward Veith, Jr. *Postmodern Time: A Christian Guide to Contemporary Thought and Culture* (Wheaton, IL: Crossway Books, 1994), p.18.
4. Dennis McCallum, *The Death of Truth* (Minneapolis, MN: Bethany House Publishers, 1996), p. 38.

Chapter Four
The Creation of Diseases

Today, Americans turn to psychological cures as reflexively as they once turned to God. But our relationship to the psyche appears to have exceeded that of believers and become more like that of cult members. An almost slavish devotion to psychological health and emotional problems dominates our culture.
Eva S. Moskowitz, *In Therapy We Trust*

Creators of the DSM-IV insist that all of the symptom clusters and categories are scientifically established. This is simply not true. Just as the stellar constellations are mythical creations of human perception, so are the DSM's diagnostic groupings.
Robert A. Baker, *Mind Games*

See to it that no one takes you captive through philosophy and empty deception, according to the tradition of men, according to the elementary principles of the world, <u>rather than according to Christ</u>. For in Him all the fullness of Deity dwells in bodily form, and in Him you have been made complete, and He is the head over all rule and authority.
Apostle Paul, *Colossians 2:8-10 NASU*

Creating Mental Illness

Labeling sin as sickness is seen nowhere more clearly than in the fields of clinical psychology and psychiatry. From the world's perspective, clinical psychology and psychiatry are the answer to the mental and emotional problems of man. The word "psychology" actually means "<u>the study of the soul</u>." Sigmund Freud, in what was lauded as breakthrough scientific exploration, cast aside the study of the soul and redefined psychology in terms of human behavior. Freud placed practical theology in the crosshairs of psychology through his underlying premise that man's problems are based *in* man and are solved *through* man and man *alone*. He knowingly or unknowingly created a religion around man with theories that are in direct opposition to God's word. Today's mental health industry is largely built upon Freud; some 250 to 450 counseling theories are in practice worldwide. They are either directly Freudian, built from underlying Freudian philosophy or are built in opposition to Freud. How did Freud come to all of his theories?

Freud graduated in 1881 from the University of Vienna with an M.D. His medical research was in the area of neurology, specifically analgesia with cocaine and opium, to which he became addicted. He was considered at one time for a Nobel Prize in medicine for his work. In 1886, funding to further his experiments became scarce. As a result, he set up a private practice and began working in the area of psychiatric counseling, hypnosis and dream analysis. To Freud, every action held some significance, and beginning his practice on Easter Sunday was certainly symbolic of his hatred for religion generally and Christianity specifically. Freud referred to himself as a "completely godless Jew" and a "hopeless pagan."[1]

The first use of "psychoanalysis" was seen in Freud's writings in 1896. The center of Freud's theory of man was: "Man is an instinct-ruled beast dominated primarily by the drives of sex and aggression."[2] Psychoanalysis grew out of and around this theory and involves delving into the subject's unconscious mind (the past) in order to determine motivations for actions and behaviors. According to Freud, the ego mediated between the animalistic id and the legalistic superego. Conflict resulted in anxiety. Freud believed if man could understand his unconscious (his past), he could come to understand himself (his present). Often, an understanding of the past led to an assignment of blame on others, thereby releasing the subject from any personal responsibility (i.e., calling sin sickness). Parents, the environment, some life trauma or primitive urges were to blame for negative behavior. Clearly, victim mentality ensues, leaving accountability for actions anywhere but squarely on the individual to whom it belongs.

As a child, purportedly Freud saw his father in a scuffle with men who were allegedly Christians. When his father did not retaliate, Freud was disgusted and vowed to get even. Some believe psychoanalysis was the tool he used. Christianity was seen as an illusion...a sign of neurosis. Freud taught that man created religion to help him deal with his surroundings. He referred to biblical accounts as fairy tales and taught that religion belonged to the infancy of the race. In order for man to progress, he would have to leave religion behind. Freud did not believe man possessed a soul. He died in 1939.[3]

> "Fools say in their hearts, 'There is no God.' They are corrupt, they do abominable deeds; there is no one who does good" (Psalm 14:1).

US News and World Report recently published an article titled, "Does Therapy Work? The Growing Controversy."[4] One premise in the article is that no school of secular therapy has proven itself to be superior to any other. Psychologist Lester Luborsky and his colleagues at University of Pennsylvania liken this to the dodo bird's statement in Alice in Wonderland, "everyone has won and all must have prizes." Now if all psychotherapies work equally well, one might presume that all of these theories could be questioned. Dr. Joseph Wortis of the State University of New York clarifies the dodo-bird statement by saying, "The proposition of whether psychotherapy can be beneficial can be reduced to its simplest terms of whether talk is very helpful."[5]

Is it possible for Christians then to benefit (or at least not be harmed) from secular psychotherapies? Based on the underlying premise in all secular theories, I would argue no. Anything, including talk that leads people into *themselves* (helping the sinful self please itself) rather than into the loving arms of the Lord Almighty ultimately leads to further sin and rebellion. Sadly, people turn from the Wisdom of the Creator of the Universe to the wisdom of a fallen, created being whose "help" is based on a humanistic system. That system neither understands nor does it provide the healing that Christians are seeking. Can man's secular counsel temporarily relieve pain? Yes. Can it satisfy a deep spiritual thirst? No. *Jer 17:5*

> "Jesus said to her, 'Everyone who drinks of this water will be thirsty again, but those who drink of the water that I will give them will never be thirsty. The water that I will give will become in them a spring of water gushing up to eternal life'" (John 4:13-14).

An Industry is Born

Today's mental health industry traces it roots to psychiatric hospitals in late seventeenth century Europe and early twentieth century United

States. These institutions managed a very small number of mental illnesses, chiefly what we know today as schizophrenia, as well as severe depression and bipolar disorder…or psychotic conditions. This was the **first wave**, if you will, of modern-day psychiatry and is sometimes referred to as **asylum psychiatry**.

Toward the end of the nineteenth century, Sigmund Freud's theories of psychoanalysis were gaining popularity. What stemmed from Freud, in the **second wave** movement, is referred to as **dynamic psychiatry**. Dynamic psychiatry expanded the reach of psychotherapy into conditions believed to stem from repressed, unconscious childhood experiences and emotions. Dynamic psychiatry thus blurred the line between what was called mental illness and more-or-less normal behavior. Mental pathology was seen to co-exist with normality. A few deeply seated conditions were seen as being responsible for abnormal thinking and behavior, yet outwardly, man seemed to be normal. Moreover, dynamic psychiatry often dealt with normal problems of living, including relationships between people at work, at home, with relatives, and with the world in general. Asylum psychiatry was relegated to institutions, and the thinking and behaviors of but a few seriously disturbed individuals. In contrast, dynamic psychiatry dealt with a very large number of behavioral and psychological conditions in people who were not institutionalized and who outwardly appeared to be normal. Over time, while many Freud-related counseling theories came and went, the second wave remained in vogue for almost 80 years. In the 1960's and 1970's, however, the world of legitimate medicine began to change. Those changes would force upheaval within the field of psychiatry, placing doubt as to whether the profession could survive into the twenty-first century.

During this time, medicine was moving toward what today is referred to as an **evidence-based methodology**. This approach rejects traditional practice methods (the way we have always done it) favoring instead scientifically proven methods for the treatment of disease. While a physician's experience was still valued, it took a back seat to more scientific information. In the medical literature, large, robust, scientifically well-designed clinical trials replaced case reports. The **case report** describes one physician's observation of a single patient or of a small number of patients. Robust clinical trials, on the other hand, are carried out by several physicians in several locations. Some clinical trials are even completed in many different countries. The benefit of the clinical trial over the case report is related to reducing bias. One physician seeing one or a few patients is more likely to be influenced by personal bias compared to a large group of physicians based around the country or around the world. Thus, a physician would need to have scientific evidence (based on clinical trials) of a particular therapy instead of operating based on his gut-feeling or personal experiences (case report-like). In essence, the move to evidence-based medicine sought to remove some of the art, or subjectivity, in medicine, moving it as a whole toward a more scientific foundation.

For psychiatry, whose body of literature was largely founded upon the case-based approach, a change to the evidence-based method would be devastating. Psychiatry had struggled for decades to maintain itself as a legitimate medical specialty and a shift of this sort represented the death knell for an already struggling movement. It is not uncommon, even today, to see those in the medical profession send persons with brain diseases to neurologists, while those struggling with the intangibles, such as feelings, should see a psychiatrist. Psychiatry has been and continues to be somewhat of a step-child in the family of legitimate medicine. When the medical profession as a whole sought to become evidence based, it quite simply became change or die for psychiatry. This need for change ushered in the **third wave** of **diagnostic, biologically-based psychiatry**.

The third wave was somewhat of a step backward. Psychiatry all but abandoned the dynamic model in favor of a new, biologically based model. Moving back toward the premise of asylum psychiatry, diagnostic psychiatry sought to **categorize disorders** into a defined set of disease entities with the basic problem being a medical or biological abnormality in the brain. Different sets of symptoms or behaviors were thus representative of a disease-based diagnosis. Similar to non-psychiatric medicine, the move toward diagnostic psychiatry insured the financial engines of psychiatric medicine would continue unabated. In fact, by moving to the biological hypothesis, psychiatry was able to tap into the vast financial resources of the pharmaceutical industry for furthering biological and genetic disease-based theories and research. The watershed moment in the change process came with the publication of the Diagnostic and Statistical Manual of Mental Health Disorders, third edition, in 1980. In this book, dynamic psychiatry was put to rest and diagnostic psychiatry was born.

The Diagnostic and Statistical Manual of Mental Health Disorders

The Diagnostic and Statistical Manual of Mental Health Disorders (DSM, Fourth Ed., text revision) is a serious looking text with nearly 1000 pages of collective psychiatric and medical wisdom in the current paperback edition. Several contributors are listed in thirteen working groups devoted to a particular set of similar "diseases". These "diseases" include a range from the rather benign sounding "Anxiety Disorders Work Group" to the "Psychiatric Systems Interface Disorders (Adjustment, Dissociative, Factitious, Impulse-Control, and Somatoform Disorders and Psychological Factors Affecting Medical Conditions) Work Group". The editors acknowledge that over 1000 people and professional organizations contributed to the work. The editors note:

> "We took a number of precautions to ensure that the Work Group recommendations would reflect the breadth of available evidence and opinion and not just the views of the specific members. After extensive consultations with experts and clinicians in each field, we selected Work Group members who represented a wide range of perspectives and experiences."[7]

Working groups also contained international members in an attempt to assure no cultural biases were inadvertently included. Each working group was instructed to *arrive at a consensus* before proceeding.

The association between the American Psychiatric Association and the World Health Organization is explicitly stated with regard to their collaboration in making the DSM-IV and the international classification of diseases, tenth edition (ICD-10), medical billing system compatible.[8] The premise of the DSM is: Patients can be assigned a code corresponding to the "disease" in which they suffer. With that code, the patient can be treated and those caring for them can obtain financial reimbursement. The DSM breaks most diseases into several criteria of behaviors, emotions and mental processes…the parts. Some number of those criteria must be met over a specified period of time in order to make the diagnosis, thereby assigning the number…the whole.

The DSM has been translated into Chinese, Danish, Finnish, French, German, Greek, Hungarian, Italian, Japanese, Norwegian, Portuguese, Russian, Spanish, Swedish, Turkish, and Ukrainian.[9] Sales for the DSM and its related products totaled $22 million in 1993,

$40 million in 1994 and were estimated to exceed $80 million by the end of 2005.[10] The list of ancillary DSM-related products is lengthy. In addition, there are widely available Continuing Medical Education programs for psychiatrists and other mental health professionals that teach billing techniques or that simply explain what is in the DSM, how it was derived and how it should be understood and used. The pharmaceutical industry or the American Psychiatric Association often sponsor these programs.

Scientifically, the primary, stated benefit of the DSM is to capture, in one volume, a common set of definitions (nomenclature) useful in diagnosing and categorizing mental illnesses. Medical professionals, psychologists, counselors, occupational and rehabilitation therapists, social workers, etc., use the DSM daily for diagnostic and billing guidance. The DSM is useful in studying disease trends, such as how many people over a certain age range or from a particular part of the country have bipolar disorder or schizophrenia. The common nomenclature, making certain everyone refers to the same condition by the same name, accepted by those in the mental health industry allows for professional specialization, research collaborations and educational opportunities around a specific set of disorders. Therefore, the DSM has become a central element in the diagnosing of mental *their* illness and in the psychology industry as a whole. It is referenced *"bible"* heavily in research papers on mental illness and is taught in psychology and psychiatry textbooks as the gold standard in diagnosing mental disease. According the American Psychiatric Association, the DSM-IV-TR "…enables clinicians to identify their patients' illnesses with a high degree of accuracy and confidence."[11]

Practically speaking (though not explicitly promoted), the manual *codes for* also serves as a roadmap for navigating the world of health insurance *billing* reimbursement. Each diagnosis is coded such that it corresponds to a billable condition. Instructions are given in the body of the manual to guide mental health professionals through what is acceptable for billing and what is not. Insurance companies often require the DSM-IV's codes when mental health professionals file claims. The Health Care Financing Administration also requires the use of the codes for the purposes of Medicare reimbursement. The editors direct mental health professionals how to "code" a particular diagnosis in order to receive proper reimbursement.

The DSM has been revised a number of times since its first publishing in 1952. The original publication was heavily influenced by a system developed by the U.S. Army for use within the Veterans Administration, as well as work already done by the American Psychiatric Association. Common nomenclature, or arriving at the same name for the same condition everywhere, was the primary driving force behind the original DSM. The first edition was modeled after the ICD-6 (see footnote above) and was heavily influenced by one school of thought: Adolf Meyer's "psychobiological view that mental disorders represented reactions of the personality to psychological, social, and biological factors."[12] DSM-II offered little in material changes from the first version. The real groundbreaking DSM was revision III published in 1980. Diagnostic criteria, the multiaxial system, and other "new" features were added. Due to several inconsistencies and a lack of clarity around ICD-9, the DSM-III was revised and published again in 1987 as the DSM-III-Revised, or commonly DSM-III-R.

As a result of DSM-III and DSM-III-R, substantial (but questionable) empirical research on diagnoses was completed, leading to the necessity to revise yet again. The editors state:

> "When a review of the literature revealed a lack of evidence (or conflicting evidence), we often made use of two additional resources…data reanalysis and field trials…to help in making final decisions."[13]

Forty **data reanalyses** were conducted and many diagnostic areas were subjected to **field trials**. The reanalyses were part of epidemiological studies or other clinical studies conveniently utilized when no "better" data existed. **Epidemiologic studies** look at large populations and attempt to identify trends that can be associated. For example, an epidemiologic study of the entire population of Framingham, MA changed the way we look at cholesterol levels in the blood as they relate to heart disease. This was done by looking at cholesterol levels in people who had suffered heart attacks compared to others who had not suffered a heart attack. As a result of the Framingham data, we have become much more aggressive in treating high cholesterol in younger people because we learned just how closely high cholesterol was associated with the risk of a heart attack.

On the other hand, **clinical studies** set out to look for specific answers to specific questions. For example, a physician may be interested to see if a particular investigational drug works to lower blood pressure. The physician would design a clinical study to see if the drug worked by comparing it to a placebo (an inert sugar pill). The study would likely include a group of similar people with respect to age, sex, and blood pressure. Some people would be put on the new drug and some would be put on the placebo. Blood pressure measurements would be taken at a set of pre-determined time points. In the end, the physician could compare the results in blood pressure from those who were taking the drug compared to those taking the placebo. He could then determine whether or not the drug worked compared to the placebo.

When one looks at an epidemiologic study or a clinical study and attempts to glean something from it that it was not designed to answer, one commits a grave error in research. One cannot draw valid conclusions from studies whose design was for a different purpose. This is like mixing apples and oranges and hoping to come up with an automobile. It simply does not work. However, as stated above, it was a regular practice used in arriving at "consensus" in the development of the DSM.

In addition, unpublished data sets were used. These **field trials** were short clinical studies conducted by working group members in an attempt to answer a particular question. There are problems with this practice as well. Other medical colleagues have not reviewed unpublished data sets, nor have they undergone scientific scrutiny by the at-large medical community. Publishing the results of one's research is the goal of legitimate academic medicine. It expands the medical knowledge base as a whole and allows others who have an interest in that area to learn from the reported experience. It also gives others an opportunity to evaluate the quality of the research and how it was conducted. Bluntly, research of the quality mentioned in the DSM would not be deemed valuable in other medical specialties, nor would it be used to develop guidelines for practice. Yet again, psychiatry is held to a different standard and poorly designed and reported research becomes acceptable.

Serious questions must be raised with the use of data reanalysis, field trials, combining of data from separate studies, and the use of unpublished data sets. These are not the methods of good science. In effect, the conclusions drawn are not based on appropriately designed empirical research and are, at best, educated guesses. When a review of the literature revealed absent or conflicting scientific data, it appears the working groups simply created their own data set with which to proceed. Under the microscope of real science, this methodology would be totally discounted. Real science contains a four-step process including: observation of phenomena; collection of data; creation of a hypothesis or theory by inductive reasoning; and testing of the hypothesis by repeated observation and controlled experiments.

DSM lacks the rigor of real science. In *They Say You're Crazy*, Paula Caplan, Ph.D. (Psychology) says:

> "As a former consultant to those who construct the world's most influential manual of alleged mental illnesses, the American Psychiatric Association's (APA) *Diagnostic and Statistical Manual of Mental Disorders* (DSM), I have had an insider's look at the process by which decisions about abnormality are made. As a longtime specialist in teaching and writing about research methods, I have been able to assess and monitor the truly astonishing extent to which scientific methods and evidence are disregarded as the handbook is being developed and revised."[14]

Caplan is a specialist in research methodology and she not only questions the methodology of the research in DSM, she questions its logic in determining who is normal and who is abnormal. She says:

> "The point is not that decisions about who is normal are riddled with personal biases and political considerations but rather that, by dint of a handful of influential professionals' efforts, those subjective determinants of diagnosis masquerade as solid science and truth."[15]

Caplan goes on to quote a psychiatrist, Renee Garfinkel, a staff member of the American Psychological Association. Garfinkel attended the November 1985 ad hoc committee meeting of the Personality Disorders Work Group and was distressed with the poor quality of thinking displayed by the work group. Garfinkel said:

> "The low level of intellectual effort was shocking. Diagnoses were developed by *majority vote* on the level we would use to choose a restaurant. You feel like Italian, I feel like Chinese, so let's go to a cafeteria. Then it's typed into the computer. It may reflect on our naïveté, but it was our belief that there would be an attempt to look at things scientifically."[16] (Emphasis mine).

Donald Godwin, one-time chairman of the Department of Psychiatry at the University of Kansas states, "Like all semi-religious works, DSM...needs an exegesis."[17]

Voting (de facto consensus-building) on a diagnosis at an American Psychiatric Association meeting is not an isolated occurrence. For example, in 1973, the APA voted to stop calling homosexuality a mental disorder in the DSM-III. Interestingly, while the APA appeared to bow to the sociopolitical pressure of gay and lesbian groups by acquiescing to their demands, the deletion claim was not exactly upheld. The DSM-III contained a diagnosis of ego-dystonic homosexuality, which means being homosexual and not feeling entirely comfortable about it. Ego-syntonic homosexuality is a feeling of virtually complete comfort with being homosexual and this was omitted from DSM-III. However, in a culture that generally looks down upon homosexuals, complete comfort is likely difficult. Thus, the editors were treating as a mental disorder what was often simply a perfectly normal reaction to being mocked and oppressed. /

What is Disease...and Just What is Normal?

According to Webster's Comprehensive dictionary, disease is defined as "disturbed or abnormal structure or physiological action in the living organism as a whole, or in any of its parts."[18] In *The Role of Diagnosis in Psychiatry*, British psychiatrist R.E. Kendell says, "There is no concept in medicine more fundamental than that of disease or illness."[19] He devotes an entire chapter to say a working definition of disease is difficult to arrive upon. Kendall states instead that diseases are concepts or ideas. Therefore, waxing philosophical, Kendell concludes that disease has no material existence and can be adopted or discarded when it no longer proves convenient. Kendall argues that the issue is not whether a disease exists; rather, the issue is whether or not it is useful. ?

Dr. Thomas Szasz, a psychiatrist and well-known critic of psychiatry and author of hundreds of papers and books says of disease:

> "All too often the problem of defining disease is debated as it if were a question of science, medicine, or logic. By doing so, we ignore the fact that definitions are made by persons, that different persons have different interests, and hence that differing definitions of disease

may simply reflect the divergent interest and needs of the definers."[20]

Szasz goes on to say:

> "...the decisive initial step I take is to define illness as the pathologist defines it...as a structural or functional abnormality of cells, tissues, organs, or bodies. If the phenomena called mental illness manifest themselves as such structural or functional abnormalities, then they are diseases; if they do not, they are not."[24]

Summarizing Szasz, Janet Vice, Ph.D. (Philosophy) says:

> "Any person whose behavior is deviant or socially unacceptable as the result of a brain disorder is suffering from a neurological disease, not a mental illness. Mind is an abstract term whose referent has not yet been clearly defined and whose nature remains speculative. Unlike bodies, which can be seen, touched, and located in space, minds are inferred from bodily and linguistic behaviors."[21]

Herein lies the riddle. Is disease a real, tangible thing or is it simply an idea or philosophy? Is the term used out of convenience in order to achieve some other goal? The general population does not ask these questions. When they hear the media, respected researchers from big-name universities, the government, or other people or authorities make claims about mental illness being a disease, about chemical imbalances and neurobiochemistry, or about the latest breakthrough medication for bipolar disorder, they are certain to accept the word of the "experts." The "biological basis for mental disease" phenomenon has permeated our culture, despite there not being a single **human trial as proof**. Again, in legitimate medical practice, this approach would be wholly discounted.

Looking at the basis for disease logically leads us to question the basis for the diagnosis of a disease. Caplan says this of disease:

> "Clearly, the project of trying to define normality is extremely problematic. There seems to be no very good way to do it and certainly no way that doesn't involve sweeping value judgments, virtually insurmountable definitional and research problems, and serious dangers to those who are classified as abnormal. Unfortunately,

the people who put together the DSM do not appear to have grappled much with most of these concerns."[22]

Should we not question a book (DSM) that guides thousands on diagnosing diseases that quite simply might not even exist? The APA says psychiatrists can depend on the DSM to be an accurate diagnostic tool to help them identify *precisely* the mental diseases of patients. However, if we do not know what disease is, how can it be diagnosed, studied, or treated?

Dr. Rex Cowdry, then director of the National Institutes of Mental Health, testified before Congress in 1996 saying:

> "Over five decades, research supported and conducted by the National Institute of Mental Health has defined the core *symptoms* of the severe mental illnesses..." however, "...we do not know the causes. We don't have the methods of 'curing' these illnesses yet."[23] (Emphasis mine).

Unfortunately, what is done all too often is this: A disease that may not exist is treated with a drug whose action in humans no one really understands while the person undergoes months or years of psychotherapy with no defined therapeutic, measurable endpoints. Fifty years of research has yielded only *symptoms*, no biologic basis, no cause, and certainly no cure. Is mental illness a disease or are issues of the heart and people relationships the core issues? Could sin be to blame?

In *Creating Mental Illness*, Allan Horwitz, Ph.D. (Sociology), explores the classification of mental disorders. He says many of today's mental illnesses, according to our symptom-based system of classification, are not really mental disorders at all. Instead, they are normal responses to social stress, relationship problems, work or other problems in living, or social deviance that may be culturally supported. This is what the DSM calls Axis IV disorders. Horwitz uses the following as a definition for mental disorder:

> "A mental disorder exists when psychological systems of cognition, thinking, perception, motivation, emotion, memory or language are unable to function appropriately."[24]

Horwitz argues the presence of symptoms alone does not reflect a disorder. The symptoms must be accompanied by system dysfunction. Note that this separates from DSM where the presence of identifiable symptoms leads to a diagnosis.

Chapter one in Kirk & Kutchins work, *The Selling of DSM,* is entitled "Psychiatric Diagnosis and the New Bible". Therein, they too contrast the "new psychology" ushered in with the publication and acceptance of DSM-III with that of Freud and psychoanalysis:

> "The creators of this revolution were far less colorful officials in government agencies, professional associations, and university research centers whose motives were as much bureaucratic and political as scientific. And what is most remarkable about their revolution is that they did not discover a single new disorder, they proposed no new treatments, and they provided no new explanation for mental illness."[25]

In essence, the authors of the new psychiatry were saying their methods are based on fact, whereas those used for over 50 years were based solely on Freud's theories. However, we must again question their logic. If the research used is faulty, as stated by Caplan and others, how can the new psychiatry business claim its work is based on fact? If the rigors of the scientific method are violated again and again, at best we are dealing with educated supposition, and at worst, pure conjecture. This is the level of certainty we allow to pervade our televisions, to which we expose our children in schools, to which we subject people dealing with heart issues in our mental hospitals, and to which we use to excuse criminal behavior in our courts. The following examples from the DSM are representative.

Anxiety, Worry, and Fear

Anxiety disorders are the most common "psychiatric" disorders encountered in general medical practice and can be seen in children as well as adults. Over the course of a lifetime, up to 30% of women and up to 19% of men will experience a DSM diagnosable anxiety disorder. There are two varieties of anxiety disorder: generalized anxiety (DSM 300.02) and panic attack (DSM 300.01; 300.21). At a given point in time, up to 6% of the population suffers from generalized anxiety while 1% experience panic attack.[26] If we assume the population of the United States is 280 million souls, then almost 17 million people are suffering from generalized anxiety and almost 3 million people are suffering panic attacks. Note that the DSM often couples anxiety with worry. The DSM refers to worry as "apprehensive expectations".

The studies of physiology related to anxiety indicate changes occur in a specific brain area. However, as is the case in many "mental" disorders, whether these changes are a cause or an effect of the anxiety is unknown. Medical science would lead us to believe the changes in brain function lead to generalized anxiety or panic attack. Hence, anxiety is a disease process that can be treated medically. Increased pulse and respiratory rates, chest tightness and feelings of impending doom are normal physiologic responses to the release of epinephrine (also known as adrenaline) and norepinephrine, and are the body's answer to frightful, "panic" situations. However, what causes these chemicals to be released? If there is a brain tumor, the patient will see a neurologist. If no gross pathology can be found, the patient may be referred to a psychiatrist.

In the DSM, the diagnostic criteria for generalized anxiety disorder (300.02) are as follows:

- Excessive anxiety and worry (apprehensive expectation), occurring more days than not for at least 6 months, about a number of events or activities (such as work or school performance)
- The person finds it difficult to control the worry
- The anxiety and worry are associated with three (or more) of the following six symptoms (with at least some symptoms present for more days than not for the past 6 months). Note: Only one item is required for children.
  - o Restlessness or feeling keyed up or on edge
  - o Being easily fatigued
  - o Difficulty concentrating or mind going blank
  - o Irritability
  - o Muscle tension
  - o Sleep disturbance (difficulty falling or staying asleep, or restless unsatisfying sleep)
- The focus of the anxiety and worry is not confined to features of an Axis I disorder, e.g., the anxiety or worry is not about having a panic attack (as in panic disorder) being embarrassed in public (as in social phobia), being contaminated (as in obsessive-compulsive disorder), being away from home or close relatives (as in separation anxiety disorder), gaining weight (as in

anorexia nervosa), having multiple physical complaints (as in somatization disorder, or having a serious illness (as in hypochondriasis), and the anxiety and worry do not occur exclusively during post-traumatic stress disorder.

- The anxiety, worry or physical symptoms cause clinically significant distress or impairment in social, occupational, or other important areas of functioning.

- The disturbance is not due to the direct physiological effects of a substance (e.g., a drug of abuse, a medication) or a general medical condition (e.g., hyperthyroidism) and does not occur exclusively during a mood disorder, a psychotic disorder, or a pervasive developmental disorder.[27]

Where is the scientific, laboratory and physical examination evidence needed for the diagnosis? How does a medical professional objectively define (as in evidence-based medicine) excessive worry, worry control, feeling keyed up, easy fatigue, irritability, significant distress, impaired social...functioning, etc.? How, specifically, is it determined that someone who exhibits two of the criteria above is not anxious (or is at least not diagnosable or billable as being a 300.02), where someone who exhibits three is anxious? If the criteria are not fully met, the DSM even allows the evaluator the option of making the diagnosis via another category known as "NOS" or not otherwise specified. In essence, it says a skilled evaluator can make the subjective diagnosis regardless of whether the criteria are fully satisfied.

What does God have to say about anxiety, fear and worry? Not surprisingly, God's Word has much to say on this topic. I believe He knew this problem would plague mankind so He addressed it in many ways and in many places:

"Do not worry about anything, but in everything by prayer and supplication with thanksgiving let your requests be made known to God. And the peace of God, which surpasses all understanding, will guard your hearts and your minds in Christ Jesus" (Philippians 4:6-7).

It is important to recognize the differences between fear, worry, and anxiety. Fear is the emotion we experience when we are in a real or perceived threatening situation. Worry is an exercise of the mind created when we think about problems over which we have no control. Anxiety is a feeling of nervousness and unease that can be periodic or persistent. Anxiety is accompanied by some very real physical manifestations such as dry mouth, rapid pulse, perspiration, increased blood pressure, clammy skin and/or anticipation.

Worry is a sin, clearly and succinctly. The verses above contain two absolutes. You have no choice as to whether or not you will worry. You are never to worry; you are to pray instead. No alternatives are given and there is an expectation of obedience. Also, note that the prayer is not a simple thing. It is to be enthusiastic, precise, and filled with thanksgiving. The thanksgiving should not be for deliverance necessarily over that which one worries. Rather it should be for completion of God's will. We should instead cherish the trial and endure, moving toward maturity and completeness in Christ.[28]

> "My brothers and sisters, whenever you face trials of any kind, consider it nothing but joy, because you know that the testing of your faith produces endurance; and let endurance have its full effect, so that you may be mature and complete, lacking in nothing" (James 1:2-4).

King David is a glowing example of a Bible character who dealt with these problems. Perhaps it was due to the years he lived in hiding from Saul. Perhaps it was due to his nation, which lived in violent and wicked times. Perhaps it was a combination of many of these things. As a result, David often felt alone and abandoned. "I say to God my rock, 'Why have you forgotten me? Why must I walk about mournfully because the enemy oppresses me?'" (Psalm 42:9). One of David's greatest contributions to us in the Psalms is his example of how he dealt with his fears, worry, and anxiety. Instead of turning to his advisors and wise men in his kingdom, David turned to God time and time again. "In the multitude of my anxieties within me, Your comforts delight my soul" (Psalm 94:19, NKJV). "I sought the Lord, and he answered me, and delivered me from all my fears" (Psalm 34:4).

He described that from which he suffered and he gave it to God. David focused his thoughts on God's power, love, sufficiency and faithfulness, moving him to thanksgiving. His faithfulness to God gave him victory over fear, worry and anxiety.[29]

"The Lord is my light and my salvation; whom shall I fear? The Lord is the stronghold of my life; of whom shall I be afraid?" (Psalm 27:1). "Why are you cast down O my soul, and why are you disquieted within me? Hope in God; for I shall again praise him my help and my God" (Psalm 42:11).

Like David, the apostle Paul also had much about which to be anxious. At the time of the writing of the letter to the Church at Philippi, Paul was in prison, not knowing if he would be released or be put to death. The main thrust of Philippians focuses on joy! Why not worry? Paul knew that worry was sin.

Anti-Social Personality Disorder (ASPD)

Consider diagnostic criteria 301.7...Anti-Social Personality Disorder (ASPD). The following are to be utilized when attempting to diagnose this disorder:

- There is a pervasive pattern of disregard for and violation of the rights of others occurring since age 15, as indicated by three (or more) of the following:
  o Failure to conform to social norms with respect to lawful behaviors as indicated by repeatedly performing acts that are grounds for arrest
  o Deceitfulness, as indicated by repeated lying, use of aliases, or conning others for personal profit or pleasure
  o Impulsivity or failure to plan ahead
  o Irritability and aggressiveness, as indicated by repeated failure to sustain work behavior or honor financial obligations
  o Reckless disregard for safety of self and others
  o Lack of remorse, as indicated by being indifferent to or rationalizing having hurt, mistreated or stolen from another
- The individual is at least age 18 years.
- There is evidence of conduct disorder with onset before age 15 years.

- The occurrence of anti-social behavior is not exclusively during the course of schizophrenia or a manic episode[30]

According to Eric Lewin Altschuler and colleagues, Samson suffered from this disorder, based on their assessment of Scripture (original Hebrew) and the diagnostic criteria from the DSM. Published in the Archives of General Psychiatry in 2001, the authors conclude that Samson met six of seven criteria for the diagnosis of ASPD:

- Failure to conform to social norms (Judges 15:6, 16:1)
- Deceitfulness as indicated by repeated lying (Judges 14:9)
- Impulsivity (Judges 15:5)
- Irritability and aggressiveness (his numerous physical confrontations)
- Reckless disregard for safety of self and others (Judges 15:15, 16:17)
- Lack of remorse (Judges 15:16)

The authors reassure the reader that Samson had no evidence of schizophrenia, nor did he appear to be in a manic state.[31]

Would God have used Samson for His purposes knowing that he was a 301.7? Recall that Samson is mentioned in faith's hall of fame:

> "And what more should I say? For time would fail me to tell of Gideon, Barak, Samson, Jephthah, of David and Samuel and the prophets...who through faith conquered kingdoms, administered justice, obtained promises, shut the mouths of lions, quenched raging fire, escaped the edge of the sword, won strength out of weakness, became mighty in war, put foreign armies to flight" (Hebrews 11:32-34).

Samson appears in quite notable company here. Did he sin? Yes. One can take almost every one of the references above (the parts) and see they represent sinful behavior. Did Samson abdicate his responsibility for sin by blaming a sickness? No. Did Samson repent and did God use him? Yes. Did God reward his service to Him? Clearly, He did.

Mental Health Money

Billing, or money, is an important issue in the mental health industry as we have noted earlier. Since there are no real tests or procedures (other than electroconvulsive shock therapy), mental health practitioners make their living in a non-procedurally based environment. Mental health professionals listen and talk, with the emphasis on the former. In contrast, gastroenterologists perform endoscopies, colonoscopies and other procedures in order to improve care and to improve their reimbursement. Surgeons operate on people to remove tumors or repair damage. Gastroenterologists perform a procedure, identify a problem (i.e., a bleeding ulcer) and treat the problem either medically or surgically. Surgeons pin a broken bone. Both of these examples illustrate a defined problem and a defined end. The readily identifiable problem is fixed (ulcer or bone) and the physician is paid for the services rendered.

Mental health is different. Rarely is the problem (as defined by the DSM) ever fixed, yet the practitioner continues to get paid as long as the patient keeps returning. In effect, the gastroenterologist and surgeon have an incentive (other than good care) to fix the problem. The mental health professional has an incentive to see the problem continue so they can continue to listen…and to bill for services. Many believe this is the very reason patients can spend years enduring psychotherapy and other forms of mental health care (including involuntary institutionalization) and actually be no better than when they came under care. The conflict of interest is rarely discussed, though it is a substantial concern.

That conflict has been expensive for one of the largest private for-profit hospital chains in the nation, National Medical Enterprises (NME). In 1991, while investigating NME, Texas Senator Mike Moncrief said, "We're the first State to turn the rock over, and it's frightening to see what's crawling out from underneath."[32] In 1992, he told Congress, "…we have uncovered some of the most elaborate, creative, deceptive, immoral, and illegal schemes being used to fill empty hospital beds…. This is not just unreasonable. It is outrageous. And it is fraudulent."[33] NME ultimately underwent fourteen separate federal and state investigations and by the end of 1993 was forced to settle lawsuits totaling $740 million. The increasing complexity of each revision of the DSM, this author believes, is directly related to an attempt to further complicate the treatment environment so that perpetual mental health care, including therapy and medications, will be required. Much more on this topic will be said in the following chapter.

Authority of Scripture Over the DSM

There are five characteristics of Scripture. Scripture has authority, it is inerrant, it is clear, it is necessary and it is sufficient. "The authority of Scripture means that all the words in Scripture are God's words in such a way that to disbelieve or disobey any word of Scripture is to disbelieve or disobey God."[34] God spoke directly to the prophets of the Old Testament or He spoke through them. Likewise, Peter and Paul both acknowledge New Testament writings as Scripture (2 Peter 3:16 and 2 Timothy 5:18). We are convinced then that Scripture is absolutely truthful because God cannot lie or speak untruthfully; it is the ultimate standard of truth and therefore, our final authority; and no new scientific or other discovery will prove the Bible to be false. Scripture is also inerrant, meaning, "Scripture in the original manuscripts does not affirm anything that is contrary to fact."[35]

"The clarity of Scripture means that the Bible is written in such a way that its teachings are able to be understood by all who will read it seeking God's help and being willing to follow it."[36] Peter tells us (2 Peter 3:16) Scripture can be hard to understand, but it is not impossible for us to comprehend the teaching. This fact is affirmed throughout both the Old and New Testaments. The Bible affirms its own clarity in passages like Deuteronomy 6:6-7, Psalm 19:7, and Psalm 119:130 where it says it makes wise the simple and imparts understanding to the simple. In the New Testament, the writers often note that it takes more of a moral and spiritual knowledge than intellectual ability to understand the teachings of Scripture (I Corinthians 2:14, for example). James 1:5-6 instructs one who lacks wisdom to simply ask, and God will provide. As with Jesus' disciples, a lack of faith or hardness of the heart can blur Scripture's teaching.

"The necessity of Scripture means that the Bible is necessary for knowing the gospel, for maintaining Spiritual life, and for knowing God's will, but is not necessary for knowing that God exists or just knowing something about God's character and moral laws."[37] Scripture is not required for knowing that God exists, however. In Romans 1:19-21, Paul tells us that even without Scripture, man cannot discount God's existence because of the nature of God's created order.

Likewise, unbelievers who have no access or interest in the Scriptures undeniably have God's moral code written on their hearts (Romans 1:32). Paul succinctly lays out the need for Scripture in knowledge of the gospel in Romans 10:13-17. Jesus says, "Man does not live on bread alone, but on every word that comes from the mouth of God" (Matthew 4:4 NIV). Just as food is needed to maintain life physically, the Word is needed to maintain the spiritual life and for growth. Hence, the Bible is necessary to know God's will. While man can have some knowledge of God's will through conscience, reasoning, advice from others, or even the indwelling of the Holy Spirit, these can only give an approximation of God's will. In a fallen world where so much is distorted from its original intent, true discernment requires the Word.

"The sufficiency of Scripture means that Scripture contained all the words God intended his people to have at each stage of redemptive history, and that it now contains all the words of God we need for salvation, for trusting him perfectly, and for obeying him perfectly."[38] 2 Timothy 3:16-17 and 2 Peter 1:3-4 are helpful as we explore the question of sufficiency. We can find answers to our questions in Scripture either directly or through the principles taught. Practically, Scripture should encourage us to think, to do and to add nothing to God's Word, considering no other writings or teachings (i.e., philosophy, science, law, etc.) to be equal. Scripture should remind us to only believe about God that which is contained in its volumes and that no word from God today is contrary to Scripture. It should remind us that nothing is sin that is not called sin and that nothing is required of us that is not explicitly taught in Scripture. Lastly, Scripture leads us to emphasize what it emphasizes and implores us to be contented with what God had told us. In short, the Bible gives us everything we need to live, research, study, preach, teach, rebuke, counsel, reason, and all else while we walk this earth. In all we do the Bible acts as a beacon to guide us through happiness and heartache. In other words, Scripture is totally sufficient.

Like the DSM, the Bible captures in one volume a common set of definitions useful in diagnosing and categorizing man's struggle in life. Everyone may use the Bible. It is useful in gathering information about sanctification by categorizing our actions into groupings...sins and obedience...and the subsets contained therein. The common nomenclature accepted by those in Christendom allows for professional collaboration, research and educational opportunities around a specific set of topics and also allows for sub-specialization or development of expertise in specific areas of academics or spiritual health.

The DSM breaks most diagnoses into several criteria of actions, behaviors, emotions, and mental processes…the parts. Some number of those criteria must be met over a specified period of time in order to make the diagnosis, thereby assigning a number and, subsequently, a disease…the whole. The patient then becomes "the number" and at times patients become quite fixated (pleased?) with the fact that they "have" a diagnosed mental disorder, purportedly as a result of a disease process. In short, in the eyes of the patient, the courts and our society-at-large, the disease removes personal responsibility for the actions, behaviors, emotions, and mental processes the Bible calls sin. People sometimes seek a cure for their disease through medical means as driven by the mental health industry. This begins what is often a long and very expensive journey represented by multiple counselors, medications, little hope and little improvement:

> "…my core thesis is that each of the typical behaviors, emotions, and mental processes (the parts) is addressed by the Bible, without attaching a pseudo-scientific label as a supposed whole. Scripture does not speak about 'obsessive-compulsive disorder' as a whole diagnosis, but the Lord does relevantly and directly counsel someone who exhibits each of the behaviors that qualify one for such a label. The mental and personality disorders codified in the DSM-IV are not matters of objective medical science. Each problem has to do with the relationship of a person to God and to other human beings. What the DSM-IV diagnoses as mental disorders, Scripture diagnoses as spiritual disorders."[6]

Conclusion

From the DSM and its lists and categories, it is easy to see how our society is affected. Illnesses are created out of a list of separate symptoms and a "condition" is named. No where else in the practice of medicine is so little made into so much. No where else in medicine do we see an entire specialty built on conjecture and supposition. No where else in medicine do we see a sub-specialty encouraged over the discovery of new "diagnoses". Over 400 new "diseases" now exist, thanks to the DSM. There is little or no objective physiologic evidence for these "diseases", yet people accept the diagnosis as if it were an irrefutable scientific fact. Western culture has been forever changed by the subtle social shifts caused by the "diseasing" of human behavior.

The way we act has not changed since the time of Adam and Noah. Then, man had become so evil and God was so disgusted with his behavior, He caused the Great Flood and also reduced man's lifespan, thus sparing him from a miserable existence mired in sin. Since the Garden, man has continued to run and hide from God, shift the blame for his behavior onto others, and cover his sin so no one will see how miserably depraved he is. In the postmodern world today, man is still trying to accomplish what he failed to complete in the Garden, namely to refuse to take accountability for his actions. The DSM is the pinnacle of man's effort to date. A collection of sins or sin-related behaviors have been composed into convenient lists, labeled as diseases, explained to the lay public using fundamentally flawed research tied to unproven chemical imbalances…and the list goes on and on. Man must take responsibility for his sin before a righteous and holy God. God made us in His image. His general revelation has allowed the discovery of serotonin, norepinephrine, acetylcholine, dopamine and over a hundred more brain neurotransmitters. Drugs that may alter these chemicals are not what He gave us for the atonement for our sin. He provided His Son for that purpose. In man's wisdom, however, we have rejected that gracious and merciful gift and replaced it with an altar to self: biological psychiatry's theory of chemical imbalances.

It is no wonder that we have witnessed a severe blow to the body of Christ as a result of the DSM and the disease-oriented culture it has helped to create. Believers everywhere, in virtually every tongue, are being told by so-called experts they are sick, diseased, genetically predisposed to illness, etc. Those same believers have been led away from the language and direction of the Bible and into themselves. Progressive sanctification is a foreign concept to many today. Becoming more like Christ each day does not require medication; it requires submission, humility, reconciliation, forgiveness, and most of all repentance. It requires a steady diet of God's Word, an environment bathed in His presence, and consistent work for His Kingdom. Evangelism begins with believers becoming sanctified and developing a burden for the lost. Those wayward souls do not need more therapy nor do they need an excuse for blame shifting. What they need to nourish their starving souls is Jesus Christ, served up by His faithful servants humbly and with much thanksgiving.

Notes

1. Jay E. Adams, *Competent to Counsel...Introduction to Nouthetic Counseling* (Grand Rapids, MI: Zondervan Publishing House. 1970), p.16.
2. Richard Ganz, *Psychobabble...The Failure of Modern Psychology and the Biblical Alternative* (Wheaton, IL: Crossway Books. 1993), p.31.
3. Anon. Freud Museum at www.freud.org.uk/chronology.htm. Viewed 09/28/2002.
4. US News and World Report. May 23, 2002.
5. PsychoHeresy Awareness Ministries at www.psychoheresy-aware.org/psychwork.html. Viewed 09/17/2002.
6. John Babler, *A Biblical Critique of the DSM-IV. The Journal of Biblical Counseling* 18(1):26. Fall 1999.
7. American Psychiatric Association (APA). Diagnostic and Statistical Manual of Mental Health Disorders. Fourth Edition. Text Revision. (DSM-IV-TR). American Psychiatric Association. Washington, DC. 2000. Paperback Edition p. xxiii.
8. ICD-10 codes are assigned to diagnoses in clinical medicine. Laboratory tests and medical procedures (such as x-rays) are coded with a separate system. Prescription drugs have another code called NDC (National Drug Code). Virtually all medical diagnosis information is reduced to a code for billing and payment purposes. Hence, each diagnosis in the DSM is assigned a code that corresponds to the ICD-10 system.
9. American Psychiatric Association. Fact Sheet: Psychiatric Diagnosis and the Diagnostic and Statistical Manual of Mental Disorders (Fourth Edition), DSM-IV. American Psychiatric Association. Washington, DC. September 1997. p.3.
10. Citizens Commission on Human Rights (CCHR). Betraying Society: Psychiatry Committing Fraud. Citizens Commission on Human Rights. Los Angeles, California. 1999. p.12.
11. APA Fact Sheet. p.1.
12. APA DSM-IV-TR p.xxv.
13. APA DSM-IV-TR p.xxvii.
14. Paula J.Caplan, *They Say You're Crazy: How the World's Most Powerful Psychiatrists Decide Who's Normal* (Reading MA: Perseus Books, 1995), p. xv.
15. Caplan p. xvi.
16. Caplan p.90.
17. Caplan p.xxiii.
18. Marckwardt AH, Cassidy FG, McMillan JB (eds.) Webster Comprehensive Dictionary. International Edition. J.G. Ferguson Publishing Company. 1992(1):365.
19. Kendell RE. The Role of Diagnosis in Psychiatry. Oxford Blackwell Scientific Publications. 1975 p.145.
20. Thomas Szasz, *Insanity: The Idea and its Consequences* (New York, NY: John Wiley and Sons. 1987), p.145.
21. Janet Vice, *From Patients to Persons: The Psychiatric Critiques of Thomas Szasz, Peter Sedgwick, and R.D. Laing* (New York, NY: Peter Lang Publishing,1992), p.15.

22. Caplan p. 52-53.
23. Hearings before a Subcommittee of the Committee of Appropriations. United States House of Representatives, Subcommittee on the Departments of Labor, Health and Human Services, Education, and related Agencies, Appropriations for 1996, part 4, National Institutes of Health, National Institute of Mental Health, March 22, 1995. p.1161, 1205.
24. Allan V. Horwitz, *Creating Mental Illness* (Chicago, IL: The University of Chicago Press, 2002), p.22.
25. Stuart A. Kirk, Herb Kutchins, *The Selling of DSM: The Rhetoric of Science in Psychiatry* (Hawthorne, NY: Aldine De Gruyter, 1992), p.7.
26. Goldman L., Bennett JC. (eds.). Cecil Textbook of Medicine 21st Edition. WB Saunders Company. Philadelphia, Pennsylvania. 2000. p.2051.
27. APA DSM-IV-TR p.476.
28. Jay E. Adams, *The Christian Counselor's Commentary...Romans, Philippians, I&II Thessalonians* (Hackettstown, NJ: Timeless Texts,1995), p.177.
29. T. Clinton (ed.), *Personality Profile...David: The Anxieties of a King. The Soul Care Bible...New King James Version,* (Nashville, TN: Thomas Nelson Publishers, 2001), p.1568-1569.
30. APA. DSM-IV-TR. p.706.
31. Altschuler EL. Did Samson have Anti-Social Personality Disorder? Archives of General Psychiatry 2001. 58(2):202-203.
32. Talley O. Legislator assails psychiatric centers; hearings planned. The Dallas Morning News. October 3, 1991.
33. Montgomery D. Moncreif testifies on need to combat psychiatric abuse. Fort Worth Star Telegram. April 19, 1992.
34. W. Grudem, *Systematic Theology: An Introduction to Biblical Doctrine,* (Leicester, Great Britain: Inter-Varsity Press. 1994), p.73.
35. Grudem p.90.
36. Grudem p.108.
37. Grudem p.116.
38. Grudem p.127.

Chapter Five
Chemical Imbalances: The Cause of Sin?

Psychiatrists maintain that our understanding of mental illnesses as brain diseases is based on recent discoveries in neuroscience, made possible by imaging techniques for diagnosis and pharmacological agents for treatment. This is not true. The claim that mental illnesses are brain diseases is as old as psychiatry.
Thomas S. Szasz, *Pharmacracy*

Wouldn't it make more sense to say that the Bible is authoritative on the spiritual realm, and the brain sciences are authoritative on the brain? It may sound plausible, but such a compromise solution actually demeans the God of Scripture and exalts human insight.
Edward T. Welch, *Blame it on the Brain*

Since you died with Christ to the basic principles of this world, why, as though you still belonged to it, do you submit to its rules: "Do not handle! Do not taste! Do not touch!" These are all destined to perish with use, because they are based on human commands and teachings. Such regulations indeed have an appearance of wisdom, with their self-imposed worship, their false humility and their harsh treatment of the body, but they lack any value in restraining sensual indulgence.
Apostle Paul, *Colossians 2:20-23 NIV*

Our worldview shapes the way we look at every situation in life. It is how we take stock of the world around us. It is the lens with which we see or interpret that which is happening in the world, our family, and our local Church. Our worldview sometimes changes over time as we learn or as new discoveries are made. For example, we may not be in favor of stem cell research because of our belief in the sanctity of human life. However, our view of stem cell research in general may change as we learn the differences between using embryonic stem cells (requiring the destruction of a human being) versus umbilical cord blood or adult stem cells (not harming a human life). Our view can change as we learn the important differences between these scientific procedures.

Moreover, as Christians, the God-directed process of progressive sanctification is a lifelong spiritual journey by which we become increasingly more like Christ. Our worldview changes as we grow in true biblical wisdom. Our view of a particular doctrine may change as we study Scripture, for example. Consider a certain monk's change in worldview almost five-hundred years ago. Through studying the Scriptures, particularly the book of Romans, Martin Luther's doctrinal worldview was altered in such a way as to begin the Reformation. His new found worldview, shaped and sharpened through the centuries, forms the basis for many of our traditions today. Luther rightly divided the Word of God and found his worldview lacking. Convinced of the sufficiency of Scripture (*sola scriptura*), he challenged the status quo at the time and, under the guidance of Almighty God no doubt, his change in worldview led to a turbulent but necessary time within the Church.

Worldview is impacted by many independent sources and we must guard against unbiblical thinking in our own development (sanctification). The influence of parents, peers, culture (the world), science, personal life experiences (the flesh), and many other sources can subtly shift our orientation away from the Word. "Defocusing" on God and all of His perfect attributes allows the enemy to creep in through the back door. This was the case in the Garden. The serpent twisted God's own Words, Eve yielded, and mankind fell. She lost her focus on God and sin resulted. While God provided the Way for man's sin shortly thereafter and subsequently gave us His Word, the devil has continued (even today) to operate his wildly successful campaign of twisting God's Word and directing man away from God and toward confusion and destruction.

The work of the devil is the root of all that is twisted and ungodly. It is said man struggles with the world, the flesh and the devil. The devil is indeed the prince of this world and he has systematically deconstructed God's design based on his own desire to be a god. The first recorded sin in the Bible was the sin of pride and self-exaltation. The Angel of Light, Lucifer, was cast from Heaven for his self-focus. Two passages of Scripture, Isaiah 14 and Ezekiel 28 were directed toward the Kings of Babylon and Tyre and these passages give us the account of the fall of Lucifer and the beginning of Satan the accuser. Lucifer fell, not only because he put himself before God, but also because he desired to elevate himself above God.

Lucifer, the protector of God's throne, said in his heart five "*I will's*", all directly related to self-exaltation and pride. Found in Isaiah 14:13-14, Satan willed to ascend into Heaven, to exalt his throne above the stars of God, to sit also upon the mount of the congregation, to ascend above the heights of the clouds, and to be like the most High. He was placing his will over that of the Father. Lucifer desired to set himself up as *the* standard and his desire was the first sin in our recorded history. As stated in Isaiah 53:6, he went his own way.

Likewise, man chooses to go his own way, oftentimes denying the Father of worship, freely placing self above all else. There are not degrees of gray, as the world would lead us to believe. There is God's way and there is man's way; there is Truth and there is conjecture; there is submission and there is pride. It was the exaltation of self, fueled by unquenchable pride, which was the beginning of evil in an otherwise perfect universe. This same lie was recycled once again in the Garden and led to the Fall.[1]   *chemical imbalances*

Today, Satan is re-using the same old lie in a variety of new and improved packages, one of which is biological psychiatry's theory of chemical imbalances. The chemical imbalance theory of biological psychiatry lands at the crossroads of medicine, philosophy, and theology. At its core, the theory is comprised of a set of presuppositions contrary to biblical Christianity. As biblical counselors, we understand something about presuppositions. We know these foundational beliefs undergird or form the foundation for our worldview.

By looking into the presuppositions (worldview) of the often quoted chemical imbalance theory, we have concluded there are at least three pillars of the chemical imbalance movement. These include first, an **absolute reliance on the theory of evolution**; second, a **belief that man is naturally "good"**; and third, an **overwhelming influence of the love of money**. As Christians, we reject the theory of evolution, not only because there is ample scientific evidence to do so, but also because it is unbiblical. Likewise, we reject the belief man is inherently good because of the doctrine of total depravity. Lastly, we recognize fully the love of money is the root of all kinds of evil.

Theory of Evolution: Pillar One

The chemical imbalance theory fully embraces the theory of evolution, thus reducing man to a complex, though fully explainable set of chemical reactions. These biological and genetic processes alone are thought to explain personality or temperament, thought processes, social deviance and all manner of man's bad behavior. A properly functioning brain, where all the chemicals interact as they should will result in a "normally" behaving human being. A person exhibiting "abnormal" behavior is thought to have an abnormally functioning brain, either due to what he has inherited from his parents (genetics), because of an emotional injury during childhood, or because of some recent traumatic experience in life. Normalizing the brain chemical milieu through medications should result in improvements in behavior and a return to "normalcy" by correcting the abnormally functioning brain.

Research in brain chemistry is completed in laboratory animals and the results are extrapolated to human beings. As a result of the theory of human evolution, people are regarded as simply the highest of the evolved species on the planet. Animal brains are less developed, but the chemical interactions are *thought to* be similar enough to draw meaningful conclusions. Notice the phrase *"thought to."* This seemingly inconsequential phrase is found throughout the biological psychiatry literature, either directly quoted or indirectly inferred. Every drug used for psychiatric conditions contains, within its FDA labeling, this or similar statements. The medical and pharmaceutical communities simply do not understand what is happening in the mind of man, nor do they understand how the drugs work. The "hard science" of what is wrong with the brain is based on animal studies as are the studies regarding the effects of drugs.

The preface of the 2004 *Textbook of Biological Psychiatry*, edited by Pankseep, explicitly states:

> "Indeed, some of the most interesting research on *mind, brain, and behavioral relations* has been emerging from animal research conducted in departments of

> psychiatry and neurology. This is a tradition in which
> all the three giants...Emil Kraepelin, Adolf Meyer, and
> Sigmund Freud...to whom we dedicate this volume
> were immersed at some point in their illustrious
> careers"[2] (*Emphasis mine*).

Mind and behavioral relations are regarded as equivalent to research on the brain. Mind is an abstract term, unidentifiable as a distinct anatomical "part" and behavioral relations describe how we interact with one another. These two "areas" are listed alongside the brain, a physical organ. Biblically speaking, we would link "mind" to "heart", and we would describe our model for behavioral relations as the Great Commandment:

> And He said to him, "You shall love the Lord your
> God with all your heart and with all your soul and
> with all your mind. This is the great and foremost
> commandment. The second is like it, you shall love your
> neighbor as yourself. On these two commandments
> depend the whole Law and the Prophets" (Matthew
> 22:37-40).

To the biological psychiatrist, these three are a continuum. What goes on in the brain IS the mind and behavior is the result. If a drug makes an animal behave in a certain way, it will likely do the same in a human.

Notice, there is no implicit or explicit mention of a soul. Man is simply regarded as the most evolved animal on planet earth. He shares some 97% of his DNA sequence with a chimpanzee, thus man must be simply a more evolved animal. The mind of man is inconsequential to the biological psychiatrist as it is simply an outgrowth of the interaction of various chemical and electrical impulses in the brain, based on man's genetic make-up and his various life traumas. Not surprisingly, the biological psychiatrist has no regard for sin. He is only concerned about diseases that alter brain chemistry causing unacceptable or bizarre behavior.

Man is Not a Rat: Refuting Pillar One

Much good work has been done by scores of biblical scholars and Christian scientists challenging the theory of evolution. However, central to the discussion of chemical imbalances is the reliance on animal data, both for behavioral and pharmaceutical research. As described above, the evolutionists see man as simply a highly evolved animal. He is the pinnacle of evolution; the very best billions of years of random mutations and survival have to offer. As a pharmacist, I have no difficulty with using animals for research in concrete areas of medicine. Animal data is very useful in a broad array of diseases from cancer to high blood pressure to arthritis. Yet there are problems in using animals for research on the mind and behavioral relations. As a conscious being, man is different than the animals. Evolutionists have attempted to say man is the same as the animals because some animals use tools, some animals communicate with one another in various ways, and some animals live in complex social structures. However, animals lack speech and from the creation account and elsewhere, we can see man is different because he is made in the image and likeness of God. The animals are placed under man's dominion and are subservient to him. Animals do not possess the image and likeness of God and they are not equipped to commune with their Creator.

At one point, the words "image and likeness" were linked to intellect and morality, respectively (see Genesis 1:26-27; Genesis 5:1; Genesis 9:6). However, a more accurate rendering of the Hebrew finds the words complementary to one another as opposed to being separate meanings. Scripture is silent on the exact qualities within a human that represent the image of God. However, man possesses a spirit and God is a Spirit. Man has an intellectual and moral nature whose essential attributes include reason, conscience and will. These attributes distinguish man from all other creatures on the earth, including laboratory rats and mice. Man is different and he has been so since his creation. God's image and likeness describes what man is, not what he has or what he does. It is what gives man the ability to think, reason, contemplate, and make decisions based upon an analysis of our options and their consequences.

The very nature of man–what I would call his mind or his "heart"– is made in a loosely similar way as God (image and likeness). It is an indwelling quality present in all humans, whether or not the individual worships or acknowledges God. All men possess an inherently religious nature. Only man worships God, whether that god is the sun, the self, mother earth, Allah, Jehovah, or someone/something else. The animals have no such desire, nor do they spend their lives searching for what only Christ can provide. This feature alone sets man apart from even the higher apes. Medical therapies suggesting a biological basis for the mind or the "heart" whose foundation is formed upon data from animals is flawed in the most fundamental way. While human hearts and livers may function in a similar way as those of animals, man's "heart" is something he alone possesses.

The image and likeness similarities between man and God were created in Adam and were no doubt altered, but not lost, at the time of the Fall. Man became twisted away from God, though he still remained rational and able to reason with a conscience and his own will. Possession of the image and likeness are not conditional, nor does one person hold a greater amount than another. Looking at Colossians 3:10 and Ephesians 4:24, we can see a change in man through regeneration. The regenerated man bears the effects of indwelling Truth or Knowledge in that he possesses positional righteousness and holiness, thanks to Christ's finished work on the Cross. He becomes conformed to the image of the Son through salvation. Thus, utilizing animals to infer the attributes of the mind or "heart" of man, or to attempt to generalize man's behavioral relations with other men, is not a valid process scientifically or theologically.[3,4]

Hence, the first pillar of biological psychiatry's chemical imbalance theory falls.

Doctrine of Man: Pillar Two

A wide plank in the center of biological psychiatry's chemical imbalance platform is the humanistic understanding that man is inherently good. Man does not commit murder because he is evil; rather, he commits murder because his brain is not functioning properly. Man has a disease known as Oppositional Defiant Disorder (O.D.D.) and could not control his explosive outbursts. Perhaps he was suffering from a post-traumatic stress disorder related flashback? Perhaps the way he was treated as a child gave rise to the development of a genetically predisposed narcissistic personality disorder? Normal people do not commit murder so she must have been overcome by temporary insanity due to her bipolar mania or her raging paranoia. Whatever the cause, the behavior was not really his fault because he has a brain disease, a chemical imbalance. Right and rational people simply do not act in such a manner.

As we have seen, man now has no need for such outmoded concepts as sin. Personal responsibility has abdicated the throne of man's heart in favor of a scientifically invalid concept. In today's modern world, all unacceptable behavior can be addressed by just the right cocktail of medications targeting the right set of neurotransmitters and receptors. In essence, modern psychiatry believes it has discovered the cure for sin, and that cure does not even begin to acknowledge the real cure: Jesus Christ. A little tweak of serotonin here and a bit less norepinephrine there and everyone is happy and feeling wonderful. It is becoming shockingly similar to Huxley's *Brave New World*. In that classic book, there was no religion, no god, and when conflicted, man simply took a gram of *Soma* to assist in reorienting his thinking. When man had a problem with living, he simply medicated his problem until he felt better. While the underlying problem did not disappear, all man cared about was feeling better in the moment.

Considering man as basically good ignores Genesis 3. The Fall of man is not viewed with credibility or authority. Without the Fall, there is no original sin. Man's feelings reign supreme. With no Fall and no sin, there is no need for the Bible. If man is good, he has no need for Christ. All religion becomes irrelevant. Man searches *within himself* for the solutions to his problems and psychology is there to provide the answers.

Conceived in Iniquity: Refuting Pillar Two

The belief that man is good is not something newly arrived upon. While the humanists may take credit for "secularizing" the concept, it is the religious community who initiated the argument. What became known as the Pelagian heresy originated in a spirited debate on the subject of free will between the Bishop of Hippo, Aurelius Augustine and the monk Pelagius. In the argument, Pelagius affirmed human nature as good and insisted sin did not change man's goodness. Pelagius' desire was to protect the doctrine of free will, meaning man either obeys God or sins according to his own free will. Adam was given a free will. It was not affected by the Fall and Adam's sin was not imputed to all of mankind. Thus, there is no original sin. Man chooses whether or not he will be sinful and he is not inclined toward good or evil. In essence, Pelagius asserted we are all born with the same nature Adam possessed prior to the Fall.

Augustine argued for the universality of man's sin. Man is born in sin and he does not have the ability to choose *not* to sin. Adam's sin is imputed to all mankind. No man is righteous in and of himself. He does not begin as a righteous being at his conception and he would die in an unrighteous state, but for the grace of God. Thus, man is completely corrupted, wicked, and wholly depraved. Sin has affected all of man including his body, his mind, his will, his ability to reason, his knowledge, his relationships and on and on. Man can do nothing "good" apart from God. While he may "do" acts of kindness, his heart is desperately wicked. Unsaved man is a child of the devil, rebellious toward God, blind to God's Truth, corrupted beyond saving and utterly helpless to save himself from the wrath to come. He is dead in his sin and a slave to his depraved nature. Regarding free will, with such a sinful nature, man simply cannot choose good over evil. While he is free to choose, his choices are limited by his nature. Man does not possess the same free will Adam possessed prior to the Fall in that Adam had the ability to choose good or evil. Once sin was imputed to the rest of mankind, the ability to choose good was lost.

Pelagius was condemned at the Synod of Carthage in 418 A.D. and subsequent Church councils have upheld Augustine's views. However, the debate on these issues has flowed freely over the centuries pitting one group against another. Even today, the question seems to be even more important because of the acceptance of the tenants of the Pelagian heresy by elements of the secular community. Humanistic psychology evolved many theories in the 1900's based on man's goodness, and as we have moved into the 21st century, biological psychiatry continues along in the same vein. The influence of these groups on the Church of Jesus Christ has been profound. Today, overwhelming numbers of evangelicals believe, that at his core, man is good.

In Jesus' time, a group of people known as the Pharisees also believed they had achieved sinless perfection; that they were inherently good by virtue of their birthright and their works. In their fallen state, they did not see their own sin, even as the Messiah interacted with them frequently. Today, God's Holy Spirit interacts with us even more frequently than Jesus did with the Pharisees, and yet man today is just as blind. One of the ways the devil keeps man deluded is by keeping him focused on his feelings and his comforts. 1 Timothy 6:10 says:

> For the love of money is a root of all sorts of evil, and some by longing for it have wandered away from the faith and pierced themselves with many griefs.

Let us look at man's love of money with respect to the biological psychiatry / chemical imbalance theory and see if this is indeed the case.

Interesting, but not unreasonable connection

Money: Pillar Three

The third pillar of the chemical imbalance theory is, quite simply, the love of money...and the numbers are staggering. There are at least three main interest groups involved in the money game, including mental health practitioners, advocacy groups, and the pharmaceutical industry. While there are well meaning people, even Christians, working in each of these fields, the overarching story is one of greed, corruption, lies, and subterfuge all in the name of providing good care to "sick" patients.

The Mental Health Machine

The chemical imbalance theory has had a shocking impact on our world. This is why we should be concerned about another medical theory. It is estimated over 40 million adults suffer from a diagnosable mental disorder each year in the United States alone. In 2002 there were 40 million visits to office-based physicians for mental disorders and 2.5 million hospital discharges for the same overall diagnosis. The same year, there were 31,655 deaths by suicide. In 2003, almost 4 million people visited an emergency room for mental disorders. All of the people behind these statistics are thought to have a malfunctioning brain as a result of a lack of serotonin, too much norepinephrine, a simple imbalance of the two, or some other conjecture to explain their behavior. Some of those people are Christians and they are all crying out for help. By and large, the Church has refused to accept the responsibility to deal with these "disorders" in a biblical fashion, preferring to refer God's people to the "professionals". Alternatively, the Church has embraced secular cures offering up "Christianized" 12-step programs, recovery workshops, classes on divorce recovery and discipleship training around coping skills.

Under our collective noses, almost 20 million American adults have an anxiety disorder of some type. Four million people have generalized anxiety disorder and over 3 million have agoraphobia, or fear of fear. Over 2 million adults have a panic disorder while 19 million have a DSM diagnosable depressive disorder. Over 5 million adults have a social phobia, 5 million have post-traumatic stress disorder, 4 million children have ADHD, 3 million adults have an

source #6 pg 104

obsessive-compulsive disorder, 2 million have bipolar disorder, and over 2 million Americans have schizophrenia.[5]

It is estimated that the burden of illness, in dollars, from all mental health disorders exceeds that of all cancers. Who is handling all these patients? As the DSM grows, so do the number of people who are sick. Eventually, the system must respond by fielding more mental health care providers. It certainly has. Between 1970 and 1995, the number of mental health professionals quadrupled. People enter the mental health system and are on a perpetual carnival ride. They get sicker and sicker but they cannot get off the nightmare. Billions of dollars of research, millions of hours of counseling, increasing numbers of diagnoses, a nearly bottomless pipeline of drugs…and not a single illness has been cured. Cancers can be cured, broken bones can be set, infections can be eliminated, once-fatal inborn abnormalities can be corrected, and not one single mental illness can be cured. Once diagnosed, people are always sick. We never hear the term recovering ulcer sufferer, but one cannot listen to the evening news without hearing about a recovering addict of some sort of another. Psychiatry is not in the business of curing. It is in a perpetual business of generating appointments, sessions, prescriptions and the next theory to explain man's behavior. The only cure offered by the mental health profession occurs after the person's insurance benefits are exhausted. Miraculously, they are cured when they can no longer pay.

Pharmaceutical Industry Influence

Between 1985 and 1994, the number of prescriptions written for mental health diagnoses increased from 33 to 46 million.[5] Thanks to the chemical imbalance theory, drugs are the therapy of choice for those millions mentioned above. In 2003, the top 200 drugs by dollar volume amounted to $152.5 billion in the United States alone. Thirteen percent of that amount or just over $20 billion dollars was spent on psychiatric drugs. More striking, when we look at just the top 20 drugs, accounting for almost $55 billion alone, $12 billion dollars was spent on psychiatric medications.[6]

Sales of drugs to treat mental illnesses are a huge business. Prescription antidepressants alone netted almost $10 billion worldwide for pharmaceutical companies in 2001. The industry advertises to consumers directly and spent billions on those efforts during the same period. One cannot watch television for an hour or flip through a magazine without seeing ads for this or that drug. How many of us have seen the cartoon of brain chemicals depicted as cute round unhappy faces? The commercial leads the public to believe there is precious too little serotonin in the brain and, because the brain has the low serotonin disease, they are depressed. Ironically, as with most cartoons, this one too is fictional, or at the very least, its basis is not in humans. In the winter, we will begin seeing ads about seasonal depressive disorder. The number of ads for depression will increase as the holidays approach as this is known to be a time when more depression is diagnosed.

In addition to the consumer ads, literally *thousands* of highly motivated, well-compensated, well-trained, and well-funded pharmaceutical sales representatives carry the message of anti-depressants to both primary care and psychiatric physicians every single day. (By far, primary care physicians are the principal writers of antidepressant prescriptions, so they receive the bulk of attention from the various drug companies.) These sales people are very well compensated, many earning a six figure income considering benefits and other "perks". The companies also provide each sales person with a budget for buying physicians meals or other entertainment. Sales people facilitate some or all of the following: Continuing education programs, dinners for physicians (under the auspices of continuing medical education), office lunches for the staff, free drug samples, pens, pads, beanie babies, cookies, car washes, free gasoline, and other items completely unrelated to the practice of medicine, in hopes it will be their drug chosen when the physician writes a prescription. After all, the sales people are provided a salary, but the real money comes in the bonuses earned based on the volume of prescriptions "their" doctors write.

With respect to education, does this not appear somewhat like the fox watching the hen house? The pharmaceutical companies are in large part providing the money for continuing education programs through universities or advocacy groups (like the American Psychiatric Association). Though they are allegedly not influencing the education provider, this is not the case. While there is nothing in writing, many of the grants are completed with a wink and a nod. The providers know if they wish to keep receiving grants, they must provide speakers and educational materials favorable to the company paying the bills.

In addition to the direct sales and educational approaches, the pharmaceutical companies hire physicians as "advisors" and pay them for giving their opinions about the latest advertising materials or marketing strategy. Oftentimes, these meetings are held in lavish resorts with first-class airfare, gifts, spa treatments and rounds of golf included. Grants are given to key medical opinion leaders in academic centers to conduct small "research" studies. Foundations, consumer groups, and associations are well-funded with pharmaceutical company generated charitable grants in hopes their work will continue to raise awareness and ultimately drive patients to their physicians.

So goes the vicious circle of events: the pharmaceutical companies pay to raise awareness by advertising directly to consumers hoping they will seek care from their physician. The physician, who has indulged in at least some of the excesses of the pharmaceutical industry sees the patient and prescribes the drug. The patient "feels" better and continues to see the physician and to take the drug. Indeed, the business of mental illness is a big business. According to Sydney Walker III, M.D.:

> "The American Psychiatric Association is literally built on a foundation of drug money. Millions of dollars of pharmaceutical advertising money are poured in the APA's publications, conferences, continuing education programs, and seminars."[7]

At one point, the American Psychiatric Association created a task force to study the feasibility of proceeding without support from pharmaceutical companies and concluded it would not be able sustain itself without drug money. The subsequent, though quiet influence of the pharmaceutical industry:

> "…has focused on expanding the number of 'psychiatric disorders' recognized by the APA, and the number of drug treatments recommended for these disorders. After all, every DSM 'diagnosis' is a potential gold mine for pharmaceutical firms."[8]

Is Taking a Mental Health Drug Sinful?

For Christians, guilt, worry, fear, anxiety, depression, anger and many other non-organic uncomfortable feelings or bothersome emotions are simply human or fleshly avoidance responses to failures to heed

God's conviction for some sin or a pattern of sin. Alternatively, the feelings may be the work of the Holy Spirit directly, as He strives to get our attention. What then can be said about the use of psychoactive medications in the treatment of these non-organic feelings and emotions? How can we draw a parallel between God's Word and medication use? Clearly the medications available today can lift depression, reduce anxiety, blunt guilt, stabilize mood, control angry outbursts and make us *feel* better. Quite simply, dare we only address feelings when heart issues are the central problem? Dare we act to chemically dull the work of the Holy Spirit? Dare we quiet that still small voice of internal conviction and risk external affliction or worse?

pharmakia
pharmacy

"Now the works of the flesh are obvious: fornication, impurity, licentiousness, idolatry, sorcery, enmities, strife, jealousy, anger, quarrels, dissentions, factions, envy, drunkenness, carousing, and things like these. I am warning you, as I warned you before: those who do such things will not inherit the kingdom of God" (Galatians 5:19-21).

A close look at this passage will allow for a more definitive answer to the questions above. The passage begins by listing the works of the flesh, translated from the Greek word *sarx or sarkos*. *Sarx* means,

"...the evil and fallen state of the soul, no longer under the guidance of God's Spirit and right reason, but under the animal passions; and they are even rendered more irregular and turbulent by the influence of sin; so that man is in a worse state than the brute: and so all-commanding is this evil nature that it leads men into all kinds of crimes..."[9]

The sins of the flesh may be categorized into four groups, according to this passage. The first set is specifically the sensual sins of adultery, fornication, uncleanness, and lasciviousness. These are followed by religious sins, namely idolatry and sorcery. The third class includes temperamental sins such as hatred, strife, divisions, heresies, envyings, and murders. A fourth class includes drunkenness and revellings and can be expanded further (...*things like these*.).

In the Greek language the word for sorcery translates into the English word for pharmacy (*pharmakia*). The word refers to the use of medicine, drugs, spells or poisons. In sorcery, drugs were often used in combination with incantations to occult powers or in the provision of magical amulets or charms. While the spell was designed to ward off evil spirits, it was also part of the mystique of the sorcerer.[10] While it would seem a discussion of drugs, illicit or legitimate, would occur here, this author suggests that it belongs with the category of drunkenness, based upon the *heart attitude* of the individual.

The Greek word *methai* (translated drunkenness) is used in the scripture above and means "intoxication." Webster defines intoxication thusly, "to poison, by bacterial toxins, serum injections, drugs, alcohol, etc."[11] Therefore, drunkenness in English applies not only to the common meaning with the drug alcohol, but also to other substances. Note that Webster does not differentiate between illicit and prescription drugs. The use of what we deem illicit drugs (heroin, marijuana, methamphetamine, lysergic acid diethylamide (LSD), phencyclidine (PCP), cocaine, etc.) would seem to easily fit into the fourth category with drunkenness. There were obviously no prescription drugs in Paul's time, but we do know from Scripture that both Paul and James approved of the legitimate use of medication as long as the heart attitude was correct. ?

Thus, the key question for us involves the heart attitude of a Christian seeking help. Is the Christian seeking a legitimate therapy to treat a documented biologic anomaly or is the Christian seeking a drug to avoid the pain of God's conviction or trial? The (non-organic problem generated) feelings psychiatrists and others seek to dispel with therapy and medications offer the Christian an avoidance strategy. If a Christian shakes his fist at God, ignoring the voice of the Holy Spirit to repent, and seeks chemical means to ameliorate guilt, anxiety, worry, or non-organic depression, he sins. He is avoiding resolution of the problem God's way. He has a God problem, not a medical problem and certainly not a disease. He is fully responsible and accountable for his sin. His past has not sinned, he has. Until he repents before God, the Lord will continue to discipline him. Therapy will never make him well. *I agree !*

Biological psychiatry offers no opportunity for repentance before a Holy and Righteous God and drugs simply cover the problem, addressing our feelings rather than the underlying spiritual pathology. For comparison purposes, consider a patient with a massive bacterial infection where his fever is treated with Tylenol®, but no antibiotics are given to address the reason for his fever (infection). The symptoms are treated, leaving the underlying problem unaddressed. In the case of so-called mental illness, the symptoms are treated and the underlying cause is left unattended. For Christians with these types of problems, honoring God and doing what He says in His Word is always a better strategy than Listening to Prozac®.

The Chemical Imbalance Theory in Depression

At the time of the initial discoveries of the psychotherapeutic drugs, little was known about brain chemistry. Throughout the 1940's and 1950's the debate was between the "sparks and the soups". The sparks were those scientists who believed the brain functioned based on electrical impulses. The soups were an emerging group of scientists who believed the brain functioned by chemical means. During this time period, new drugs were being discovered and they seemed to have some positive effects in seriously ill mental patients. However, no one really knew how the drugs worked, nor did they really understand what was going on either physiologically or psychologically in their patients.

Real credibility for the chemical basis of information transmission in the brain occurred in the early 1960's when a group of Swedish chemists and pharmacologists discovered a method for identifying serotonin, norepinephrine and dopamine in the brain. This, and other animal data from rats and lower primates, led to the SPECULATION that psychoactive drugs MIGHT modify neurotransmitter activity AND mental disorders MIGHT result from either an excess or a deficiency of some neurotransmitter activity. Could part A be true without part B being true?[12]

In 1965, two influential articles were published out of the National Institutes of Mental Health concluding the cause of depression was an abnormal functioning of brain biologic amines (neurotransmitters). Much of this research was based upon work done with a blood pressure medication, reserpine, which was thought to cause depression. It was later discovered that reserpine does not bring on depression in most people. It does appear to cause more depression in those already depressed, however. Thus, if the underlying hypothesis is flawed, the research conclusions built upon the hypotheses are likely to be flawed as well. If the conclusions are based on the reserpine data, they are not valid conclusions. Over the years, there has been much speculation as to which neurotransmitter is the most important in depression. The tide has shifted from norepinephrine to dopamine to serotonin. What we now know, however, is that there are over 150 neurotransmitters in the brain. Still, we all seem to be talking about those researched 50-60 years ago. Considering what we have learned about neuro-pharmacology, it is indeed amazing how little the biochemical theories of mental disorders have changed over the last half-century. In *"Blaming the Brain: The Truth About Drugs and Mental Health"*, Elliott Valenstein says:

> "The evidence is clear that none of the proposed biogenic amine theories of depression can possibly be correct. In the past the appearance of a convincing argument for one of these theories has resulted from selecting only the evidence that fits and ignoring that which does not. The various biogenic amine theories are often discussed in review articles and textbooks as though they were basically true, except for a few facts that have not yet been adequately explained. There are few rewards waiting for the person who claims that "the emperor is really nude" or who claims that we really do not know what causes depression or why an antidepressant sometimes helps to relieve this condition.... We are currently in a position where it is clear that none of our theories is right, but we do not know what to replace them with. In the meantime, there are a number of groups that have their own reasons for promoting the theories and glossing over their serious deficiencies, rather than admitting that we really do not know what causes mental disorders or why the drugs are sometimes helpful."[13]

In essence, while some facets of science have moved forward in attempting to explain the chemical soup in our brains, the research has been limited by the cracking foundations of the pillars upon which it is built. The electrical, or "sparks" theories have been all but abandoned, yet electrical activity in the brain is measurable and useful to legitimate physicians. Neurologists who treat epilepsy rely heavily on the electroencephalograph (E.E.G.) for therapeutic decision-making. How can the psychiatrists discount the electrical theories of brain activity while neurologists rely heavily upon it? Many questions remain regarding the biological basis of mental disorders.

Cause and Effect

Now, let us address an oft raised question. What if, sometime in the future, science gives us the ability to assess chemical interactions in the brain? Will that not then prove, once and for all, we are simply a complex set of chemical reactions functioning in a unique environment created over billions of years of stellar and biological evolution?

The answer quite simply is no. Correlation does not prove causation. Because we "discover" low serotonin concentrations at nerve junctions in the brain, does not mean, definitively, low serotonin causes depression. Low serotonin, in theory only, may be related to depression...but why is there low serotonin? How do we know what is low and what is "normal"? Is low serotonin genetic? Is it a result of some other thought or feeling or behavior? Could it be caused by what we are thinking and how we are behaving or our responses to certain situations, such as stress? Could it be related to the medications or foods or pollution or mosquito bites or bacon or artificial sweetener or red dye #3, or magnetic fields from electrical power lines, or one's religious affiliation....you get the picture. If we are able to locate a particular biological marker associated with a given alleged mental disorder, it is tempting to say the marker is the cause of the disorder. However, this is not a scientifically valid argument. In fact, Valenstein states:

> "There is no reason to assume that any biochemical, anatomical, or functional difference found in the brains of mental patients is the cause of the disorder. It is well established that the drugs used to treat a mental disorder, for example, may induce long-lasting biochemical and even structural changes, which in the past were claimed to be the cause of the disorder, but may actually be an effect of the treatment."[14]

We know, for example, stress can actually alter the function of the brain (animal data), along with increasing certain adrenal gland hormones like epinephrine, norepinephrine and cortisol. Repeating certain tasks *over and over* can also lead to structural changes in certain neurons in the brains of animals. Moreover, experience can alter neuronal structure. It is not a stretch to think repetitive thoughts and behaviors may also affect the brain's physical structure. In fact, human brain activity can be shown via PET scan to change with cognitive psychotherapy (talk therapy) or behavior modification activities. At the risk of extrapolating animal data to humans, I believe there may be a correlation between this concept and the biblical counseling concept of habit. Address a sinful, habitual pattern of behavior biblically and brain activity is likely to change. It also leads me to not gloss over the concept of *renewing one's mind* while putting off sin and putting on the new man (Ephesians 4).

Renewing the mind is sometimes lost during the course of counseling as it is somewhat overshadowed by the put-off/put-on process. Bathing the mind in Christ via personal Bible study, corporate Bible study, ministry activities, and being surrounded by godly people, I am convinced, is necessary for true change to occur.

that is what I did... saturated my mind with Scriptures !

Concluding Remarks

Scientifically, the chemical imbalance theory is discussed as if it were fact, though there are many, many issues challenging its validity. Its presuppositions are decidedly unbiblical, like a house built on shifting sands. And it is fueled by massive financial interests. God's people are being led astray. However, the battle for truth is not a new one for us. While the tactics may change, the strategy is no different today than it was in the Garden. God's goodness, faithfulness, character and providential care for His children are being questioned and, as Adam and Eve, man continues to fall short.

While we have made great strides in medical research over the past 100 years in particular, any scientist will say our understanding of the function of the human being is minimal. Our understanding of the mind of man is equally poor. Each time we "discover" something...the cure for a disease or the answer to a research question...the discovery itself creates additional questions. Soon, we realize truly how little we know for certain. Christians must begin to appreciate the awesome complexity of the universe, and the power and majesty of an immense God who created it all in the span of only 6 days. We must come to understand the fact that God knows us infinitely better than we know ourselves. He provided for us a guidebook for life. Why should we not utilize it fully in discovering how to deal with our problems?

Earlier we noted that our worldview can change based on learning and sanctification. We must realize what is going on around us outside the Church. Discernment is of paramount importance or we will never stop ~~the yeast from contaminating God's unleavened bread~~. As we come alongside other believers, counseling them, discipling those who will, helping them see God's Word more clearly, let us be unwavering in our commitment to God's goodness, faithfulness, character and His love for us. The old lie is the same. It has been in use since Eden. God has entrusted this generation with His Church. It is an awesome responsibility, but one with great rewards. As you who are counselors dispense hope to counselees, let us also take hope in the fact that He has equipped us for the work at hand and He will not fail us.

Notes

1. J.Vernon McGee, *Through the Bible with J. Vernon McGee. Commentary on Isaiah and Ezekiel* (Nashville, TN: Thomas Nelson Publishers, 1982).

2. Jaak Panksepp, *Textbook of Biological Psychiatry* (Hoboken, NJ: Wiley-Liss, 2004), p. xix - xx.

3. Charles Hodge, *Systematic Theology* Volume II: Anthropology, Chapter 5: Original State of Man. Hendrickson Publishers, Inc. reprinted from the edition originally published by Wm. B. Eerdmans Publishing Company, June 2003).

4. Millard J. Erickson, *Christian Theology (2nd ed.).* (Grand Rapids, MI: Baker Books, 2004).

5. National Institutes of Health. National Institute of Mental Health, *The Numbers Count: Mental Disorders in America.* 2001. Viewed at http://www.nimh.nih.gov/publicat/nimbers.cfm 08/01/2005.

6. Anon, *Top 200 Prescriptions for 2002 by U.S. Sales.* NDCHealth, NDC PHAST. 4/2004.

7. Sidney Walker III, *A Dose of Sanity* (New York, NY: John Wiley & Sons, Inc., 1996) p.229.

8. Walker III, p.230.

9. Adam Clarke's Commentary. Biblesoft 1996. Electronic Database. PC Study Bible v3.2F. 1988-2001.

10. Wycliffe Bible Commentary. Moody Press 1962 Electronic Database. PC Study Bible v.3.2F. 1988-2001.

11. Marckwardt AH, Cassidy FG, McMillan JB (eds.) Webster Comprehensive Dictionary. International Edition. J.G. Ferguson Publishing Company. 1992(1), p.667.

12. These statements were forever joined at the "AND". Perhaps the drugs do have some effect on brain chemistry. Perhaps the mental disorders were indeed a result of either an excess or deficiency of a particular chemical. Shockingly, even today, neither of these statements is supported by solid science. Both are considered truth in the psychiatric community and by the public-at-large, chiefly because we have no other theories upon which to rely. Millions of adults and children are being used as sophisticated laboratory animals because we have no idea what is "wrong" with them physiologically (if anything), nor do we have any idea how the drugs we are giving them actually work.

13. Elliott S. Valenstein. *Blaming the Brain: The Truth About Drugs and Mental Health* (New York, NY: The Free Press, a division of Simon & Schuster Inc., 1998). p.102, 94.

14. Valenstein p.126.

Descent into Deception

Psychology is displacing the role of the church in modern Christianity. I do not believe that this is the conscious purpose of most Christian psychotherapists, but nonetheless it is happening.

> Dr. Ed Bulkley, *Why Christians Can't Trust Psychology*[1]

To the degree to which the Christian who counsels holds to one counseling model or another, depends not so much upon background and training (though that certainly plays an important part) but more so as to how strongly that Christian views the authority of the Bible and its adequacy as a "Handbook" for the human mind. Otherwise, the individual's Christian faith becomes merely a general format over which any given number of psychological concepts may be superimposed.

> Dr. Dennis Frey, *Biblical Directionism*[2]

Your boasting is not good. Do you not know that a little leaven leavens the whole lump of dough?

> Apostle Paul, *I Corinthians 5:6*

The state and condition of the church was of primary importance to our Puritan forefathers, not because they had retreated from the world, but because they believed the state of the church determined and regulated the state of society. These champions of the faith possessed a religious rationale for every decision. That belief set them apart from everyone else as a sanctified group of people. In their day, many were looking for political, economic, or other reasons for crime, abuse, poverty, immorality, and so on, but to the Puritan, sin was the only explanation. Consequently, there was no more important question than, "How are things going with the church?" Today, we should be asking the same question in the same context as our Puritan forefathers.

What is the state of the church today? Unfortunately, it is not a hard question to answer. Statistics tell us church membership has been steadily decreasing year after year. Sunday school, which was once popular, has also been declining in attendance. Prayer meetings, missionary groups, and fellowship meetings in general are weak and feeble. Because of poor attendance, many churches today have cancelled mid-week and Sunday evening services altogether or have limited preaching in favor of other activities where the activity is the focus and the gospel is absent or only alluded to by association. Megachurches are growing in prominence but they are generally marketing driven entities short on doctrine and long on a feeling orientation. Thus, the church as a whole is declining in attendance and in its knowledge and commitment to Scripture.

Another question must be asked if we are going to fully understand the condition of the church today. What about those who still go to church? While some have abandoned the church altogether, we console ourselves with the fact we are faithful to the services and meetings. We go to Sunday school. We regularly read our Bibles. As such, we have a tendency to measure ourselves against those who are unfaithful or sporadic church attendees or those who are unreligious altogether. We measure ourselves by a standard of man while the true standard is the New Testament. Do we shine forth as lights in the world or do we blend into the world so well, no one can see our light? Is our zeal and enthusiasm for Christ apparent or are we motivated by legalism or self? Is our zeal for Christ as strong as our zeal for our job or our zeal for our children or our zeal for our golf game...? Do we give people the impression all our religious activity is a matter of duty or a matter of pure joy? Do we have life in us? Do we genuinely have a burden for souls? Do we mourn and pray over the state of the world? Do we satisfy and justify ourselves by "attending church" and keeping things going? Are we as earnest as Christ's enemies? Is our faith in the gospel message equal to or greater than the faith in the message of those who oppose Christianity? Do we realize the state of the church is very different from what it was fifty years ago, or even twenty years ago? What has happened? Why is the church in such a deplorable condition today?

There have been many explanations put forward and we would agree they all have a certain amount of influence. However, the primary reason scores of people are no longer attending church is the church's departure from the authority and sufficiency of Scripture. When men believed in the authority and sufficiency of the Scriptures, Christianity flourished as God blessed the church. However, in the mid-nineteenth century, a movement to replace divine revelation with man's philosophies arose. Man's ideas and his ability to understand his world through science, philosophy, and psychology became the new standard. The wisdom of man replaced divine revelation. Modern science and education discredited the old beliefs so people retreated from the Bible as the banner of absolute truth. Christians talked more about the preacher's scholarship, knowledge of science and psychology rather than piety and knowledge of biblical doctrine. Doctrine was seen as divisive and, as such, was no longer important or emphasized. At the same time the authority of the Bible was being attacked; men like Darwin and Freud were being lauded. The church was well on its way to compromising the teachings of Scripture in favor of modern views. It was in this context that psychology, with its plethora of schools and theories began to shape the church, shifting its beliefs away from the Word.

Beginning in the mid 1950's, with an ever increasing number of books being written on the subject, evangelicals made friends with psychology. Psychology was touted as an adjunct to and servant of the faith. Properly appropriated, psychology would enhance pastoral ministry and induce spiritual growth and maturity. Christian psychologists asked, "How can we apply Scripture to an individual when he does not even know himself?" Psychology would supposedly give man insights about himself so he could then apply the right Scripture. However, the theory had hidden problems. Self became the focus and the servant psychology became the master. The attempt to integrate psychology with Christianity turned into an overt psychologizing of the Christian faith.

One of the first well-known Christian psychologists was Clyde Narramore. It was Narramore who popularized the trichotomist theory of human nature. He allocated each part of man to a professional. The medical doctor cared for the *body*; the psychotherapist cared for the *soul* (he helped people with emotional and psychological problems); and the pastor cared for the *spirit* (salvation). The trichotomist theory legitimized the psychologist to the evangelical. Consequently, several institutions were founded to train clinical psychologists and integrate Christianity with mental health services. The Christian Association for Psychological Studies (CAPS) was founded in 1956 by a small group of Christian mental health professionals. Fuller Seminary of Psychology, whose slogan is "the cross in the heart of psychology", is considered the founding center for the study of Christian faith and psychology. Fuller is the oldest seminary-based clinical psychology department and was the first clinical program outside a university to receive American Psychological Association (APA) accreditation.

Bible-believing evangelicals became one flesh with professional psychology in the 1970's. Christian counseling and psychotherapy became a legitimate calling for those who wanted to go into ministry, but did not want to become a pastor or missionary. Bible colleges and seminaries of every denomination increasingly offered evangelicals the education they needed to become licensed clinical psychologists. In 1973, a group of Christian mental health professionals at Rosemead Graduate School of Psychology began exploring the integration of Christian faith and psychology, establishing the Atlanta Clinical College. Later they partnered with a state university to offer training and research within a Christian context. This organization, with campuses in Atlanta, Georgia and Chattanooga, Tennessee became known as the Psychological Studies Institute. In 1977, Wheaton College in Wheaton, Illinois established a masters program and in 1993 a doctoral program in psychology. Moreover, some of today's most popular Christian psychologists were prominent faculty members at other conservative seminaries. For example, Frank Minirth and Paul Meir were at Dallas Theological Seminary; Gary Collins was at Trinity Evangelical Divinity School in Deerfield, Illinois; Larry Crabb was at Grace Theological Seminary in Winona Lake, Indiana; and Clyde and Bruce Narramore founded Rosemead.

Integration was the key word for this growing professional community of believers. Books and articles laid out the agenda. Psychology was necessary to better understand the nature of man and his behavior. Theology was necessary to accurately interpret psychology by separating the chaff of error from the wheat of truth. The two would mutually stimulate the other. Under the general guidance of Scriptural principles, they would profit from psychological data, institutional arrangement and practice. It was likened, by psychologist Larry Crabb, to when the Israelites plundered the Egyptians of their silver and gold.[3] What they all failed to recognize was the biblical principle of being unequally yoked. They failed to see the error of mixing the leaven with the unleavened. The Bible teaches in 1 Corinthians 5:6 and Galatians 5:9, integration of even a small amount of leaven ruins the whole lump of dough. Despite these teachings, the integration movement gave the church an unnatural but intellectual rationale for linking together evangelical theology and psychology. It also provided a network for professionals and institutions to carry out their practice of what became known as Christian psychology, Christian psychotherapy or Christian counseling. Satan was again successful at twisting God's Word.

By the late 1980's, psychology had inundated every aspect of Christian life. Psychological categories increasingly became the language of daily life. In sermons, Sunday school classes, Bible studies and homes, words like self-esteem, damaged emotions, unconditional love, dysfunctional families, support groups, intervention, codependent and felt-needs seeped into the Christian vernacular. The words were changing in a subtle but powerful way. In seminars, conferences and on the radio, Christian psychologists were filling the roles once held by theologians, pastors and Bible teachers. Psychologists, not pastors, were considered the experts when it came to people and their problems. The psychologist became the authority for defining right from wrong, good from bad, and constructive from destructive. Support and twelve-step groups evolved from what once had been Bible study or prayer groups. Bible exposition was downplayed and the focus of evangelicalism was on feelings, emotions, hurts, old wounds, repressed memories, meeting psychological needs and recovery. Springing up all across the country were Christian in-patient clinics of which Minirth-Meir and Rapha were the most notable. At the same time, small groups in churches were created and provided support to individuals and their families. In many instances these small groups fed people into larger clinics or provided after-care for those who were discharged.

What is an Evangelical?

Running in parallel to the development of psychological theories in the church, was the evolution of the meaning of the evangelical church, itself. As we have stated, the meaning of words changes over time and from culture to culture. Word meanings are somewhat fluid and do evolve as the people using the words change. Lexicographers are those who study these changes and assist us in determining the original meanings of words. This practice is central to our understanding of the Bible as it was written many hundreds of years ago by men living in substantially different cultures than ours. Does the Word today mean what it did 2000 years ago? Has it changed drastically, delicately or not at all? Interpreting Scripture based on the historical-grammatical method utilizes the science of lexicography. Scholars involved in Bible translation must consider this as they render the original languages into not only English, but also every other language in use today.

Using the methods of lexicographers, we can discern the meaning of the word *evangelical* and see how it has changed over time. The root word is the Greek *evangelion*, or *evangel*, and is the word translated "gospel" in the New Testament. Thus, we could render the word evangelical to mean one who shares the gospel or is a "gospeler." While the word evangelical ultimately embraced a broad array of people with differing views on many doctrinal areas, it was held together with the glue of two fundamental doctrines. Evangelicals believed in the authority of Scripture (inerrancy) and in justification by faith alone. Thus, evangelical became simply another term for Protestant. Beginning in the nineteenth century, even this began to change.

A result of post-Enlightenment modernism, a social gospel began to take hold. Attention was turned from a personal God and a personal relationship with His Son, to a focus on social and cultural rebirth. The term evangelical was then further narrowed to represent one who believed in a personal faith through individual salvation, rather than through a societal or cultural renewal. Personal, one-on-one evangelism became a hallmark of the mid-nineteenth century evangelical. Thus, evangelical became tantamount to evangelistic. What evolved was a liberal agenda of a social gospel contrasted with the conservative agenda of personal evangelism. Fast-forwarding a hundred or so years takes us into the mid-twentieth century and a realization of the error of separating social concerns from personal concerns. Up until this time, the definition of an evangelical was narrowing. However, realizing now the error of separating social and personal concerns, the ranks of evangelicals, by definition, swelled to great numbers! In other words, the definition of evangelical became more narrowed, while those who defined themselves as evangelical grew dramatically.

Just when it seemed things were going to settle, more challenges to evangelicals emerged, both from within and outside the Church. In the 1960's, social unrest and overt attacks by the secular humanists were in full force against the Church of Jesus Christ. The Bride was *we lived* being attacked externally from multiple angles including: feminism, *through* the sexual revolution, social reforms, normalization of divorce, and *this* destruction of the traditional family, to name but a few. Internally, the *change* attacks were more subtle and were a response to the external pressures. We were more interested in "sweet fellowship" with those harboring different sets of core beliefs (doctrine) than Scriptural accuracy. As a result, doctrine was sacrificed on the altar of a "feeling" oriented gospel; a desire to feel good about ourselves as the Church superseded our points of doctrinal difference.

At the same time, the church was fighting another internal battle due to influence from liberal theologians. A groundswell of condemnation for the **inerrancy** of Scripture rose to a fevered pitch. As a result, some compromised and accepted a so-called middle position of **limited inerrancy**. Others deserted completely by adhering to a position of **infallibility**. As inerrancy was one of the two main doctrines of traditional evangelicalism, what was once a word encompassing many had again become a word describing the few.[4] While many today still refer to themselves as evangelicals, as we trace the meaning of the word, we see clearly there are few evangelicals as the word was originally defined. Evangelical has become a loose word, tossed about by many, including the media, but truly understood and practiced by a small minority.

As a result of the confusion, the groundwork was laid for the psychologized church. Is it not interesting to look back and see how well organized, planned and executed Satan's plans have been? Working multiple angles with multiple objectives, Satan has sewn lies and confusion and is reaping mightily. The psychologized church is alive, well and growing.

Does Psychology Have a Place in Evangelicalism?

The short answer to this question is no. However, let's look briefly at the why. A root argument goes back to Martin Luther's two kingdom perspective. Luther, and later Calvin, asserted there are two kingdoms. The first, ruled over by Law and representing God's power, is the kingdom of natural man. The second is the Church, ruled over by the Gospel and representing God's grace. In the first kingdom, natural man may be both "good" and evil. Man can and does perform acts of kindness and compassion, as seen by the world around him, and God can reward those acts in this life. Man may also be wicked and utterly despicable. God may or may not punish him in this life for these evil deeds. However, the concept of "all have sinned" applies to the first kingdom. Despite man's kindness and "good" deeds, he is still separated from God by his sin and cannot perform enough good deeds to offset his sin.

It is the kingdom of God's power, or the Law, where psychology and related fields belong. Psychology seeks to understand why natural man behaves the way he does. Why indeed do some people live upright moral lives while others commit heinous crimes against one another? Psychology and the other social and medical sciences seek to understand differences in man's anatomy and physiology, genetics, environment, upbringing, culture…all aimed at ascertaining his feelings, thinking, and behaviors. Thus, these scientific and pseudoscientific disciplines strive to determine cause and effect in the natural world. Why natural, unrighteous man does what he does, considering the natural world around him, is the aim of psychology.

By definition then, psychology has no place in the kingdom of grace. Grace is the kingdom of righteous man, made so by the blood of Jesus Christ. Applying the principles governing unrighteous man to righteous man is doomed to fail, leading to confusion, frustration and spiritual stagnation. While some of the principles used in the multitude of psychological counseling models may lead to superficial improvements in righteous man's feelings, thoughts and behaviors, these models only address that part of man, the flesh, governed by the Law. Paul teaches us the natural man is dead and we are to live according to the spirit. All of Romans 8 illustrates the sharp contrast between the flesh and the spirit, and we would be wise to apply this thinking to our view of God's general revelation. While all knowledge does come from God, including scientific discovery, He does not necessarily intend for His general revelation to be applied generally. The kingdom of grace is governed by the Gospel and He has given us His special revelation through the Scriptures as our guide. Applying psychological principles distilled through general revelation to spiritual man causes one to become double minded (James 1:1-8).

Why has Psychology Become so Popular in Evangelicalism?

The intrusion of psychological thought into the Church is not the "fault" of the social or medical sciences themselves. Fault lies squarely with the local church. Historically, the evangelical church has been weak in dealing with problems occurring between people. Bad or nonexistent counseling, coupled with a poor understanding of the fundamentals of theology, created a vacuum toward the end of the nineteenth century just as the fathers of modern day psychological thought were rising to prominence. The Church was mystified by explosions in the sciences and it was becoming more liberal socially. This combination naturally opened the door for the pseudoscientific theories of Freud, Darwin and others, leading to the mess we are in today.   *how the "mainstream"*
            looks at all this —
Biblical cures for relational problems are foreign to modern people. The average church-attending Christian today struggles to understand the depth and magnitude of his sin and sadly, so do many pastors. Psychiatry, on the other hand, sounds scientific and mainstream. The long disease descriptions have abbreviations and categories, and are associated with specific behaviors and medications. The words are familiar and full of present day context, thanks to advertising, talk shows, self-help books, government programs, and a psychologized educational system. While the church is talking about what are viewed as arcane problems like salvation, justification, and sanctification, the psychologists are giving out advice for the problems facing "real" people.

The areas where evangelicalism has grown weak are the very areas addressed by psychology. Where there was a gap in the teaching of the church, man filled in with his own sin-tainted wisdom. As such, psychology has the answers for family problems, addiction, mid-life crisis, anxiety over work and relationships, and other problems not immediately identifiable in Scripture. The church has been left behind when it comes to solving life's problems, and the world has moved on. In the mind of the struggling man and woman in the trenches of hour-by-hour life, the church has become irrelevant. Does the Bible not rightly deal with these issues? Is it any wonder Christians are confused about sin and sickness?

Our problems are all the same. We sin. Yes, there are a multitude of sins and even more ways of sinning by commission or omission. However, all have sinned and sin is sin. In God's eyes, telling that little white lie or committing genocide renders one ineligible for Heaven. Sin brings death, no matter what the sin. We all sin and we do it habitually, regularly and often. While the method of sin may be different from person to person, the nature of the sin is the same (1 Corinthians 10:13). In the loosest sense, sin is a disease; it is the plague of mankind by which we were infected by our parents. The Bible has the prescription antidote for sin. The Bible is a counseling textbook. All counseling issues are theological issues because all of life is lived before God. Wherever man is, God is. Solomon wrote: "The eyes of the LORD are in every place, watching the evil and the good" (Proverbs 15:3). All attitudes and behaviors at all times are lived out before the Lord. Man simply cannot lift himself out of his theological context. Anger, bitterness, envy, deceitfulness, lying, gossip, and rebellion are common issues in counseling. These are also spiritual issues. Just as the theory of evolution tries to lift man out of his theological context, so does psychology. Evolution attempts to explain how man got here without God. Psychology attempts to explain why men behave as they do without God. It is unbiblical to treat problems of living as though they are unrelated to God. Paul wrote, "For we must all appear before the judgment seat of Christ, that each one may be recompensed for his deeds in the body, according to what he has done, whether good or bad" (2 Corinthians 5:10). The Apostle also warned:

> See to it that no one takes you captive through philosophy and empty deception, according to the tradition of men, according to the elementary principles of the world, rather than according to Christ (Colossians 2:8).

"Rather than according to Christ" is the fatal phrase which Paul used to describe the system of doctrine that had found its way into Colossae. It was a philosophy that set up the wisdom of man in opposition to the wisdom of God which has been the root cause of every human problem. "Man's wisdom," over the centuries, has taken many different forms, such as the present church-growth movement. It has varied with time and culture, but it has always been there in one guise or another to displace Christ's sufficient Word with man's wisdom.

For a multitude of reasons, some mentioned above, the Church has allowed the wisdom of natural, unrighteous man to creep in through the back door. Some have welcomed him and have left the door open for more. Some closed the back door only to let him in through the front. Few have refused him. The result has been the emergence of a new kind of church, one that is devoted more to pleasing the natural man than God. – *"man-centered"*

Psychologized Neoevangelicalism

The newest form of evangelicalism sweeping communities across the nation is the so-called seeker-sensitive church. In the past, evangelicalism was grounded in sound doctrine and a clear purpose. Today, the new evangelicalism is driven by business model consumerism, complete with sophisticated, psychologically-based marketing, advertising and market research. The end goal is to build larger and larger congregations, becoming what is known as a megachurch. In these organizations, the gospel is marketed and sold to a community as if it were a shiny new car or boat. Music, drama, plasma screens, small groups, coffee houses and the like appeal to many as the god of entertainment has replaced the God of Abraham. Preaching is exclusively positive and encouraging, as a direct descendant of Robert Schuller's possibility thinking.

This is the pop-church era. Community survey based felt-needs (ala Schuller, Hybels and Warren) guide church organization and programming. Psychologists are replacing pastors on Christian radio (Focus on the Family) as they host call-in programs heavy on psychobabble and light on Scripture. In the pulpit, lip service is given to Truth while doctrine is eroded away due to avoidance of anything remotely resembling controversy. Forgiveness and tolerance are preached and taught far and wide, but the stark realities of following Christ are omitted. Is it any wonder this movement is sometimes referred to as "easy-believism"? The Bible is relegated to the shelf as personal experience, emotion, feelings, and popular opinion guide individuals and entire church bodies. Along this vein, many seminaries teach a psychologized curriculum to those who will be pastors along with those who will be psychologists. Consider the advertisement for a well known seminary found in a popular Christian magazine. It asks, "Read Any Good Books Lately?" The picture shows a Bible placed on top of a copy of the DSM-IV-TR. The caption below the picture reads:

"Though seemingly unrelated to some practitioners, we believe the DSM-IV and the Holy Bible belong together on the bookshelves of any future psychologist who desires to treat the whole person: body, mind, and spirit."

The foundation of faith has changed. It is no longer in Christ and Him crucified, but in man and his felt needs and emotions. Compromise reigns and pragmatism rules. If individual Christians and pastors would invest as much time and energy into evangelizing and discipling as they do in business planning and psychologizing, perhaps evangelicalism would be on a more solid footing today. Taken further, entire churches are swept into gross doctrinal error while their pastors write books and give interviews to secular publications about methodology instead of theology. God is stuffed into a box, only to be taken out when the Internal Revenue Service passes by.

The Therapeutic Recovery Church

The psychologized church of the present day generally does not advertise itself as such, though even that is changing. One can find psychologized churches within most, if not all, the mainline Protestant denominations. Psychologized churches exist as well among the non-denominational ranks, and their numbers are growing every day. What began as allowing groups such as Alcoholics Anonymous to use space in the church for their meetings has mushroomed into a fully mature movement within evangelicalism. As Paul refers to in several passages, a little leaven spoils the whole loaf. In this case, the Church invited the enemy into the camp.

In the Old Testament, when the children of Israel moved into a new land, God often instructed them to destroy everything in that land (Deuteronomy 7:1-6 and others). He meant everything…all the people, the livestock, the buildings…everything. In spite of God's warnings, His people did not always heed His Word. God knew His children would be tempted to incorporate what they had conquered into their own culture, and they did. Soon, His chosen people were no longer pure, but rather a people polluted by the very cultures they had conquered in God's name. The consequences were catastrophic and often led to judgment. Today's psychologized church has done much the same. It has allowed the leaven of psychology, man's wisdom, to infiltrate the church. It has accepted psychology's language, its excuses, its therapies…and the results have been no less catastrophic for God's people. Like the children of Israel, we have incorporated psychology's culture into the church. We have polluted pulpits far and wide with a watered down gospel where sin is called sickness.

Chief among the psychologized churches are those dedicated, in whole or in part, to recovery. On one end of the spectrum, some churches offer programs aimed at a particular segment of the population, such as divorce or "addiction" recovery. They offer thinly veiled twelve-step discipleship (recovery) programs for hurting people groups assuming this will serve as an outreach activity to an unchurched population. Other churches form small groups, not to study the Bible through sound hermeneutics and exegesis, but to act as de facto psychological group sessions where everyone feels safe discussing all their problems or "diseases." Some small groups become a surrogate priest where the member pours out his soul suffering to the group under the guise of requesting intercessory prayer. The group takes on the role of counselor offering their own insights, mostly based on personal experiences using psychological jargon and only loosely based on Scripture. Yet another faction has gone so far as to base their entire mission as a church on recovery. They include the word "recovery" in their name, often breaking denominational ties, abdicating accountability and oftentimes abandoning sound doctrine.

Recovery churches preach the gospel of the twelve-step program, inviting all those who are hurting into their congregations with the promise of love and grace as a substitute for the perceived judgment and rebuke often found in fundamental churches. Regardless of whether the church has dipped its toe in the recovery waters or jumped in head first, some degree of compromise with the sufficiency of Scripture has been made. Man's wisdom has replaced God's Word and the results have been wildly successful. Recovery is being successfully marketed by secular and "Christian" companies and alike. The Hallmark Company developed a line of "recovery" cards, bookmarks, buttons, key chains, framed prints, coffee cups, journals, magnets, T-shirts, and self-stick note pads. In addition, one can obtain the *Life Recovery Bible* in the New Living Translation thanks to leading recovery experts. Recovery has arrived squarely in the center of the main stream by catering to man's "itching ears", replacing God's wisdom with the wisdom of sinful man.

Replacement is an ongoing theme in the recovery church. The doctrine of salvation is replaced with the felt need of self-realization. Self-denial is replaced with self-love and self-mastery. Sin looses its sting unto death. The holiness of God, complete with His anger and discipline toward sin, is minimized in favor of the "grandfather" God who understands and loves unconditionally. Progressive sanctification is replaced with ongoing recovery (remember the power of words!). Focus on being a new creature in Christ is shifted to seeing my sins as lifelong imperfections. Being subjected to church discipline for unrepentant sin is thought to be too harsh and is replaced with victimization or disease mentality:

> Recovery Assertion: "Since I am a victim of my past, my problems should be expected. I should not be held accountable for my anxiety and depression."

> Biblical Translation: "Because I am self-centered and unrepentant, I still suffer from guilt, anxiety, and depression as God disciplines me. I need to be responsible before God for my actions. I need to repent, put-off this pattern of thinking, renew the spirit of my mind through the Word, and put-on righteous behavior and thinking while serving others."

God admonishes us to heed His warnings and to seek out His knowledge and wisdom. Proverbs 1:20-33 clearly illustrates how God responds. He asks how long we will love our ignorance, hating knowledge. God promises to mock and laugh at the troubles of those who ignore His wisdom, while refusing to listen to their prayers. He says they will eat of the fruit of their own way, living with the consequences of ignoring God. Their complacency will destroy them. However, to those who practice the wisdom and knowledge He freely provides, God promises to pour out His Spirit upon them, teaching them His Words. These will live securely and be free of the fear of danger.

However, in the recovery church, doctrine is minimized as people are directed to develop a deeper relationship (feeling) of love with God. Loving God takes precedence or completely overshadows being obedient to His Word. Rebuking sin is shunned while restoration is paramount. Compromise is everywhere. Evangelism is dead and sanctification is discouraged. People enter the recovery church seeking help and they find a pastor-psychologist who invites them on an emotional roller coaster they may never be able to get off. How did this happen?

The failure has been the result of theologically weak pastors and even weaker Christians, near reverence for anything medical or medically sounding, and mixing psychology with Scripture in an attempt to create a stronger prescription for healing. This integration results in compromised Christianity, powerlessness, and stagnation in growth. Who can offer a stronger prescription than the Great Physician Himself? *Amen!* *Col. 2:9 10* According to the disease model, recovery is an ongoing, lifelong process. One who was once in the grip of alcohol, for example, has the disease of alcoholism. If he is able to get sober, he will forever be recovering. Complete victory, by definition, is impossible. On the other hand, if one is a drunk, he can repent, and be forgiven. He doesn't need the twelve steps of Alcoholics Anonymous (man's wisdom); God's Word is sufficient in showing him how to put-off sinful habits and put-on righteousness. He can be completely *Rm 8* victorious over sin. He will no longer need weekly meetings to remind him he is a sinner because he is a new creature in Christ.

The issue at hand in the recovery church is that of forgiveness. Christ's finished work on the Cross allows us to say Jesus completely forgives, and He forgives completely. The therapeutic church glosses over forgiveness. Much like the mental health industry, recovery churches and perpetual church programs keep people recovering from their sickness (sin). In this model, there is no victory and no cure…only one more day of recovery. One lady who came to our office had been in a thirteen week grief recovery program for fourteen years! She is not an exception. When recovery is the focus, victory over the power of sin and guilt, which is called sickness, is nonexistent. Does this not sound remarkably similar to the mental health machine noted earlier? Does it also sound contrary to what is taught in Scripture regarding God's unconditional forgiveness of *confessed sin*? As the well known hymn asks and answers:

> What can wash away my sin?
> Nothing but the blood of Jesus…
> What can make me whole again?
> Nothing but the blood of Jesus…
> Oh! Precious is the flow that makes me white as snow…
> No other fount I know, nothing but the blood of Jesus…

The blood of Jesus is what is curiously missing from recovery programs and churches. To stay in a perpetual state of recovery denies Christ's finished work on the Cross, sets aside salvation for another gospel, and aborts the process of progressive sanctification. Believers and the Church become spiritually withered, defeated, weak and paralyzed. Why must it all be so complex and convoluted? God deals with man as either righteous or unrighteous measured against nothing more than His Word. Is man today that much more complex than he was 2000 or 5000 years ago? Requiring psychology to explain "modern" man calls Scripture inadequate, limits God's Sovereignty, and gives Satan a victory.

Conclusion

> "For if the trumpet give an uncertain sound, who shall prepare himself to the battle?" (1 Corinthians 14:8)

No subject at the present time calls evangelicals to more serious and urgent attention than the state of the church. The gap between the church and the world has never been narrower. We are in the midst of a very great battle, and the tragedy of the hour is the confusion of the Christian church with regard to it. The trumpet yielding an uncertain sound is the precise problem.

This is not the first time the church or society has been in the present condition. The advantage of studying the Bible is that one gets an accurate perspective on history. Therefore, in a sense, we are not facing anything new. However, there is a unique element in the situation the church faces today. As there have always been periods of gross sinfulness and moral degradation, the additional factor today is sin being called sickness. We are not just faced with immorality, but an outright widespread denial of sin.

The position prior to the twentieth century saw Christians as disobedient, lazy and lethargic toward spiritual matters. They did not deny the reality of sin, however. What was needed was a rousing or awakening as in the days of Whitefield and the Wesleys. This is not the case today. It is not a matter of just waking people up. A poison… psychology…is surging through the veins of evangelicalism.

The claims of psychology concerning the nature of man and his problems have not been put forward as a theory, but as fact are based totally on unproven "scientific" dogma. These teachings have become entrenched orthodoxy in the Christian church and are defended with a zeal scarcely equaled. Christians and non-Christian laymen and scientists have realized the kind of pseudo-scientific concepts foisted upon the public as it pertains to evolution, but they have yet to do so with psychology. Few in evangelicalism would deny there are serious problems within the church; but the answers given for the reasons are very different. While there may be other peripheral causes that have certainly caused problems in the past, we maintain the main cause is the denial of sin. Our present difficulties are theological, and the church itself has been mainly responsible. Man's reason and understanding, his philosophy, replaced God's revelation.

The insidious spread of psychology into the church is the reason evangelicalism counts for so little in the modern world. The church is confused concerning the nature of man and his behavior. One cannot understand the problems we face today unless one realizes that the thinking of the vast majority of Christians is governed and determined by what they regard as science. Psychology, it is believed, has the diagnosis for all our problems. Man is explained in terms of the resultant operation and interaction of various biological, chemical, and other forces. We contend this explanation has led to the present conduct and behavior of men and women, Christian men and women, included. The result is commonly referred to as "diminished responsibility". In other words, if psychology can prove scientifically a man has the disease of alcoholism, then he is not responsible for certain behavior. If a child has Attention Deficit Disorder he is not responsible for his selfishness and disruptive behavior in the classroom. The inevitable result is a drastic decline, an abdication, of morality and godliness.

Believers are failing as Christian people in their daily lives. Immorality, rebelliousness to authority, and lack of self-control are as common among Christians as they are among unbelievers. The divorce rate among Christians and non-believers is the same. Isaiah wrote, "Alas, sinful nation, people *weighed down* with iniquity" (Isaiah 1:4, italics mine). Everyone is having problems. Depression, anxiety, fears and despair are rampant. Believers are looking for answers. Tragically, most evangelical pastors and leaders are trumpeting uncertain sounds. Sin is called both sin and sickness. Lying, anger, immorality, and stealing are sins, but they are sicknesses too. Love is a virtue and a sin. Pastors and leaders are giving people mixed signals, leaving them in a state of confusion. How will they prepare for battle? When life's problems come their way where are the trumpeters pointing them? They have accepted psychology's diagnosis of man's problems and have eagerly begun practicing psychology's "cure", namely more therapy and more medication.

The psychological way of ministry has, over the years, filled the church with a mistaken sense of optimism. The label "Christian psychology" is nothing more than the theories of Freud, Rogers, Jung, Fromm, Maslow, and others. Imagine atheists and agnostics "empowering" believers for kingdom growth. The idea that man can supplement the Bible with his own ideas is the height of arrogance. The Bible was given to the church for the pursuit of its work in salvation and sanctification. The presuppositions and methodology of counseling must come from the Scriptures. However, it is argued that secular counselors may stumble over some truth that is not contradictory to the Scriptures. They contend Christians may integrate their new revelation into their counseling theory and practice. After all, "all truth is God's truth." However, if it is indeed necessary for counseling, the truth will be found a purer form in the Holy Bible.

All of God's truth is *wholly* true. Error mixed with truth contaminates the truth, making it error. The devil quoted the Scriptures, but then added his own words. The Pharisees, who possessed considerable knowledge of the Scriptures, "invalidated the Word of God" by mixing it with their traditions (Matthew 15:1-7). What they believed and taught was no longer truth, even though it was mixed with truth.

Integrating psychology with God's Word is like a buffet at a restaurant. The buffet contains a wide variety of meat, fish, vegetables, breads, and desserts. A group of believers go through the buffet, and when they return to their table, they see that everyone has a different combination of food on their plate. In the same way a group of Christians go through a buffet containing several hundred conflicting theories and models of psychology. Each person is looking for "truth." After going through the buffet, they see that they all have different "truths" on their counseling plate.

God's Word is inerrant. It is all true. An integrationist may say he has discovered "God's Truth," but how does he establish it as God's Truth? Has he received a new revelation from God? If so, it is on par with Scripture. However, man's thinking and capacity to grasp truth has been affected by sin. Though he professes to be wise, he is

[handwritten: Good page - have where we stood...]

"foolish" and his thinking has become "darkened" (Romans 1). For that reason, psychologists are constantly discarding their theories for new ones. *[handwritten: Amen!]*

The Bible teaches that all Christians have everything they need for real victory and change. Christ omitted nothing in His redemptive work. Believers are granted everything pertaining to life and godliness. The Apostle Peter wrote, "seeing that His divine power has granted to us *everything* pertaining to life [salvation] and godliness [sanctification], through the true knowledge of Him [not the strange doctrines of Freud and Rogers] who called us by His own glory and excellence" (2 Peter 1:3, italics mine). Christians are complete in Christ Jesus (Colossians 2:10).

Our sufficiency is not in ourselves and certainly not in any man. The Apostle Paul wrote, "Not that we are sufficient of ourselves to think any thing as of ourselves; but our sufficiency is of God" (2 Corinthians 3:5, KJV). Expanding on this great truth, he further stated: "And God is able to make all grace abound to you, that always having *all* sufficiency in *everything*, you may have abundance for every good deed" (2 Corinthians 9:8, italics mine). God has provided all the necessary resources we need to meet the challenges of life. Psychology has nothing to add to God.

Psalm 19 says the Scriptures are sufficient. The Scriptures are "perfect, restoring the soul."[5] What more does the Christian need? The Scriptures are *perfect*. They are complete and whole. They do not need to be supplemented by man's theories. How can human wisdom enhance perfection? The Scriptures *restore* the soul. The Scriptures are adequate for changing people's lives. The Scriptures can transform a depressed person into a peaceful and happy person (v. 8). The Bible can *enlighten* as to the cause and cure of problems (v. 8).[6] And because the Scriptures are perfect and can restore a man's soul, they are more valuable than all the theories, myths, strange doctrines, and speculations of men (v. 10).

Psalm 119 is a psalm about the sufficiency of Scripture and is full of help for counselors and their counselees. The psalmist wrote: "I have more insight than all my teachers, for your testimonies are my meditation" (v. 99, NASB). Hard as it may seem, there are many believers who delight in Carl Rogers' client-centered therapy or Abraham Maslow's hierarchy of needs. They delight in their feelings of significance and worth. As biblical counselors it is our job to point to the Word of God. The psalmist continues: "My soul cleaves to the dust; revive me according to Thy word" (v. 25). It is God's Word that will revive and change people.

Models of counseling that deny the Scriptures altogether or deny the Scriptures by denying the sufficiency of the Scriptures must be hated. The psalmist wrote, "From Thy precepts I get understanding; therefore I hate every false way. Thy word is a lamp to my feet, and a light to my path" (vv. 104-105).

Jesus prayed for His disciples, "Sanctify them in the truth; Thy word is truth" (John 17:17). There is no statement in all of Scripture that so clearly declares sanctification in its fullest sense is accomplished by God's Word. The so-called experts, secular and Christian, insist the Bible is insufficient for sanctification. The fact is that the Scriptures give us more insight into man's problems than all the experts. The psalmist declares, "I have more insight than all my teachers, for Thy testimonies are my meditation" (Psalm 119: 99).

God testifies His Word is wholly adequate for every need. Paul wrote, "All Scripture is inspired by God and profitable for *teaching*, for *reproof*, for *correction*, for *training in righteousness*; that the man of God may be adequate, equipped for every good work" (2 Timothy 3:16-17, italics mine). The sufficiency of God's Word is demonstrated in four ways: God's Word teaches truth, reproves sin and error, corrects behavior, and trains in righteousness. The Scriptures are adequate to show a person what is right, what is wrong, what he needs to do, and how to do it (i.e., how to change). *yes!*

Col 2:8

While an integrationist may truly admire the Bible, his reliance on psychology shows an equal, if not greater, confidence in secular theories and therapies. If he blends Scripture and psychology then he does not believe the Scriptures are sufficient. If the Scriptures are not sufficient then Christ is not sufficient. To maintain God's sufficiency while at the same time saying His Word is deficient is absurd. God and His Words are inseparable. It is through the written Word of God we come to understand the living Word of God.

Counseling has always been a part of the normal activity of the Church. God has given pastors and elders the task of teaching and changing people's lives (sanctification) through the authoritative ministry of His Word (2 Timothy 3:15-17). Pastors often claim they do not have time to counsel. As busy as our Lord was, He always found time to counsel individuals. Counseling was a major part of Paul's ministry. Paul wrote, "And we proclaim Him, admonishing *every man* and teaching *every man* with all wisdom, that we may present *every man* complete in Christ" (Colossians 1:28, italics mine). Notice Paul said "every man." In Acts Paul is quoted as saying, "Therefore be on the alert, remembering that night and day for a period of three years I did not cease to admonish *each one* with tears" (Acts 20:31, italics mine). Paul's ministry of the Word not only included public preaching, but "admonishing" individuals. The word admonish is the Greek word *noutheteo* from which Jay Adams coined the phrase "nouthetic counseling."[7] To admonish or warn an individual is one of the elements of Nouthetic or Biblical Counseling. There is something in the individual's life that God wants to change. Paul says he admonished individuals for their sinful behavior or attitudes. Luke further recorded Paul's words, "How I did not shrink from declaring to you anything that was profitable, and teaching you *publicly* and from *house to house*" (Acts 20:19-20, italics mine). Paul ministered the Word publicly and from house to house. Paul visited individuals and families who were having difficulties, just as people do today, and he taught them using the Scriptures. Nouthetic ministry is how the New Testament Church functioned. All believers are commanded to "admonish one another" (Romans 15:14); "encourage one another" (Hebrews 3:13); "comfort one another with these words (1 Thessalonians 4:18); "encourage one another, and build up one another" (1 Thessalonians 5:11); if a believer is caught in a sin, and repents we are to "restore one another" (Galatians 6:1). To help one another, by skillfully using and applying God's Word, is the duty of all believers.

The Bible is a book about behavior. *rooted in the realities of the gospel* To the Ephesian believers Paul instructed, "laying aside falsehood, speak truth; ... be angry, and {yet} do not sin; ... let him who steals steal no longer; ... let no unwholesome word proceed from your mouth, but only such {a word} as is good for edification; ... let all bitterness and wrath and anger and clamor and slander be put away from you, along with all malice; be kind to one another; ... be imitators of God; ... walk in love; ... do not let immorality or any impurity or greed even be named among you; ... {there must be no} filthiness and silly talk, or coarse jesting" (Ephesians 4:25-5:4, explanation added).

The Bible is *the* counseling textbook. Biblical counseling is grounded in the conviction that God has spoken about and to human beings. The Bible gives the counselor the right *presuppositions* he needs to know to counsel. Presuppositions have to do with what the counselor is to believe about God and man. The Bible gives the counselor the *methodology* he is to use to minister to his counselee. This has to do with the process of counseling. The Bible gives the counselor the *content* of counseling. What exactly does the counselor say to the counselee?

It would be impossible to understand the state of evangelicalism, and society as a whole, without taking into consideration the way it has been affected by psychology. Very few things in the history of the church have come close to matching its influence upon beliefs and practices. This is due to the fact that psychology and its techniques and practices are considered to be "neutral" and therefore not threatening to Christianity. Nothing could be further from the truth. Psychology is inherently anti-Christian, and sadly it is extensively promoted by Christians.

A model of man based on the presupposition that man's condition is the result of sickness, low-self-esteem, personality type, birth order, poor socialization, or any of the dozens of other guesses men put forward, rather than sin, is a denial of the doctrine of sin. Problems of living are God-related and always involve the fallen or redeemed state of man. Man needs the counsel of God. Man was created a spiritual being and never was intended to live independently from God. For that reason, God counseled Adam in the Garden on a variety of topics such as animals, food, idleness, work, loneliness, and his relationship to Himself and Eve. God instructed him on the importance of obedience and the consequences of sin. Satan countered God's counsel with his own. "Indeed, has God said...?" (Genesis 3:1).

Those who promote psychology, like all integrationists, cast doubt upon God's Word. They question, ignore, embellish, distort, and contradict the plain teachings of Holy Scripture. They are blind guides. They teach believers to fix their eyes not on Jesus, "the Author and Finisher of their faith," but on Sigmund Freud, Carl Rogers, and others. They lead believers to trust in man's wisdom, the hallmark of secular humanism, and doubt God's Word.

Evangelicalism has reaped what it has sown. The Judeo-Christian ethic has been weakened. Sickness, not sin, is everywhere in the church. Evangelism and sanctification have been drastically affected. Church leaders are trying to figure out the problem. Meanwhile, the

Christian patient is slowly dying and they keep giving him the same "Christian" psychology that made him ill in the first place.

In problem solving, the most basic need is to understand the problem, to characterize it appropriately, and then to apply the correct solution. This is the case in fixing a malfunctioning engine in your car, a problem with the plumbing in your home, or even more complex feats of engineering. It is also the case when dealing with issues of health. The problem, or sickness, must be accurately diagnosed before it can be treated. For example, several years ago, one of the authors suffered from chronic hoarseness. It affected his ability to speak so profoundly he sought medical treatment from his family physician. The doctor assessed his ailment as an infection and prescribed antibiotics. The problem did not improve and some time later, a visit to a specialist was scheduled. The specialist immediately diagnosed the hoarseness as being a result of ongoing bronchitis, an inflammatory condition of the upper airways. Anti-inflammatory drugs were prescribed and the hoarseness improved and ultimately resolved. Once the correct diagnosis was made, the problem could be treated with the right medication. The specialist was viewing the condition from a different perspective and arrived at a different diagnosis. The different diagnosis led to different treatment and a different outcome.

Every single day people walk into their physician's office complaining of this or that symptom and the physician treats it based on his or her perspective and training. For example, a successful Christian businessman is rushed to a hospital complaining of shortness of breath, chest pain, and an overall feeling of impending doom. These are common symptoms of an evolving heart attack. Upon a full assessment, it is decided he has not had a heart attack but he is suffering from anxiety or a panic attack. The man is discharged with a prescription for an anti-anxiety drug and an appointment with a psychiatrist. The psychiatrist looks at the diagnosis made in the emergency room and begins to work on the problem from the perspective of his unique training. Perhaps the man has a chemical imbalance? Invariably, the psychiatrist will lead the man to look into himself for the answer to his problem and so begins the man's journey on the endless road to recovery. Perhaps the man's problem is related to sinful behavior…an "extramarital affair" (adultery), embezzlement (he is a thief), an addiction (idolatry), or something else. If this is the case, he will not find the solution within himself; no matter how long he stays in therapy and no matter what drugs he takes. The psychiatrist's diagnosis is wrong and the treatment will not be successful.

The critical necessity for an accurate diagnosis of the underlying problem is fundamental to solving or curing the pathology. If the diagnosis is wrong, the treatment is likely to be not only ineffective, but also potentially dangerous; dangerous in the sense that the original problem is not addressed and the wrong treatment carries with it the potential for side effects or other unwanted results. In the example immediately above, the Christian businessman may continue to live in sin. Psychology and Worriers Anonymous will not solve his sin problem. They may help him feel better about himself, but Jesus is the only hope for his sin problem. Jesus Christ is the Great Physician who possesses the cure to the most serious, life threatening problem man faces: his inability to deal with his sin and separation from a Righteous and Holy God.

Notes

1. Ed Bulkley, *Why Christians Can't Trust Psychology*, (Eugene, OR.: Harvest House Publishers, 1993), p. 191.
2. Dennis Frey, *Biblical Directionism*, (Newburgh, IN.: GMA & Inspiration Press, 2003), p. 3.
3. Larry Crabb, *Effective Biblical Counseling*, (Grand Rapids, MI. Zondervan Publishing House, 1977), p. 47.
4. R.C. Sproul, *Faith Alone: The Evangelical Doctrine of Justification*,(Grand Rapids, MI.: Baker Books, 2002), Chapter 1.
5. Psalm 19 and 119 are psalms about the sufficiency of Scripture. It is important that every biblical counselor learns to use these psalms in defending their commitment to counseling biblically.
6. These are the same claims made by psychology thus making psychology competitive with God's Word.
7. For a further study in the presuppositions and practices of Nouthetic Counseling, see Jay Adams' books *Competent To Counsel*, *The Christian Counselors Manual* and *A Theology of Christian Counseling* published by Zondervan Publishing House.

About the Authors

David M. Tyler, a native of Illinois, has served as a pastor in Southern Baptist churches in Illinois and South Carolina. He holds a B.A. in Theology, an M.A. in Pastoral Ministry, and a Ph.D. in Biblical Counseling. Presently, Dr. Tyler is the Director of Gateway Biblical Counseling and Training Center, a ministry of Edgemont Bible Church in Fairview Heights, Illinois. He is certified by the National Association of Nouthetic Counselors and the International Association of Biblical Counselors. Dr. Tyler is the Vice President of the Board of Directors of Master's Divinity School and Graduate School of Divinity in Evansville, Indiana. He serves on the Board of Directors of Personal Freedom Outreach in St. Louis, Missouri and is a regular contributor to the Quarterly Journal. Dr. Tyler also lectures and leads workshops on Biblical Counseling. He is the author of *Jesus Christ: Self-Denial or Self-Esteem* and *Self-Esteem: Are We Really Better Than We Think?*

Kurt P. Grady is a practicing pharmacist in the St. Louis area. He earned a Bachelor of Pharmacy and a Doctor of Pharmacy degree from the St. Louis College of Pharmacy and completed post-graduate training in Clinical Pharmacy at the University of Florida Health Science Center in Jacksonville. He also holds a Masters in Business Administration from Southern Illinois University at Edwardsville. Recently, Dr. Grady completed a Doctor of Biblical Studies in Biblical Counseling from Master's Graduate School of Divinity. He serves as a deacon at Edgemont Bible Church and as a counselor and instructor at Gateway Biblical Counseling and Training Center in Fairview Heights, Illinois. Dr. Grady is an assistant editor for the Journal Christianity and Pharmacy and is a member of the Christian Pharmacists Fellowship International. He has published a number of articles on biblical counseling topics and lectures at national and regional counseling conferences.